AF615602

TEACHERS' RESOURCES

Keys to Classroom MANAGEMENT

WATERBIRD BOOKS
Columbus, Ohio

President: Vincent F. Douglas
Publisher: Tracey E. Dils
Contributors: Katherine Ruggieri, Clare Cherry, Jane E. Bluestein, Ph.D.
Project Editors: Joanna Callihan, Teresa Domnauer
Interior Design and Production: Lithokraft

This edition published in the United States of America in 2003 by Waterbird Books,
an imprint of McGraw-Hill Children's Publishing,
a Division of The McGraw-Hill Companies
8787 Orion Place
Columbus, Ohio 43240-4027

www.MHkids.com

Library of Congress Cataloging-in-Publication Data is on file with the publisher.

Printed in the United States of America.

1-57768-537-7

1 2 3 4 5 6 7 8 9 10 PHXBK 09 08 07 06 05 04 03

The McGraw-Hill Companies

TABLE OF CONTENTS

Dear Teachers,

So often the most frustrating problems associated with teaching are the basic management problems encountered every day. *Keys to Classroom Management* offers practical advice and management strategies for beginning and experienced teachers alike.

This book is divided into two sections. The first section, *Classroom Organization,* provides ideas for organizing your classroom, paperwork, communication, and routines. The second half of the book, *Behavior Management,* offers specific guidelines for helping students develop responsible behavior, solving problems, and communicating with children.

We hope this book will help you manage your classroom more efficiently, make your days run more smoothly, and present you with strategies that will add to your success as a teacher.

Sincerely,

Waterbird Books

Part I
Classroom Organization

CHAPTER ONE

Organizing Your Environment

Your classroom environment is everything that surrounds you—from bulletin boards to lunch cards. Each item needs to be well thought out and organized in order to create a comfortable, efficient classroom environment.

Desk Arrangement

Student desks should be oriented around the most frequently used chalk or whiteboard. Desks may directly face the board or be perpendicular to it. Position desks so that children are able to easily pay attention. When arranging desks, consider students' age. Some children prefer to have their own space. For example, to a first grader, having his or her own desk is a new and exciting passage which says, "Now, I'm a big kid." He or she will likely be very possessive of his or her new space. Student desk arrangement reflects your expectations of how students will interact with each other. Decide how much communication you want and arrange desks accordingly.

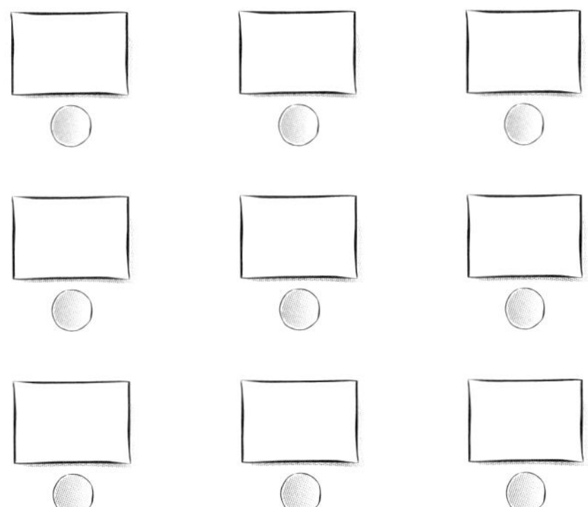

Student desks can be organized in rows. This formation will limit student communication. However, this arrangement is valuable for talkative classes. Another advantage is that students can easily pair up during cooperative learning by having alternate rows move desks toward a partner in a stationary row.

To encourage teamwork, organize student desks in tables or groups. This arrangement encourages relaxed communication. Usually a group of three to five students is best. A group of more than five usually ends up functioning as two smaller groups. Tables or groups can earn points or privileges, such as first out to recess, for appropriate behavior.

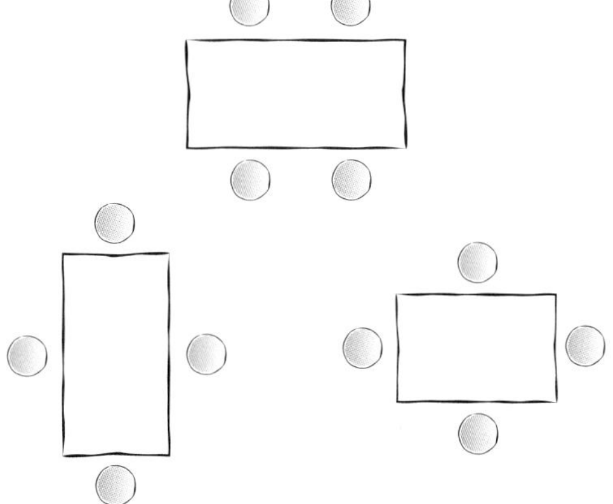

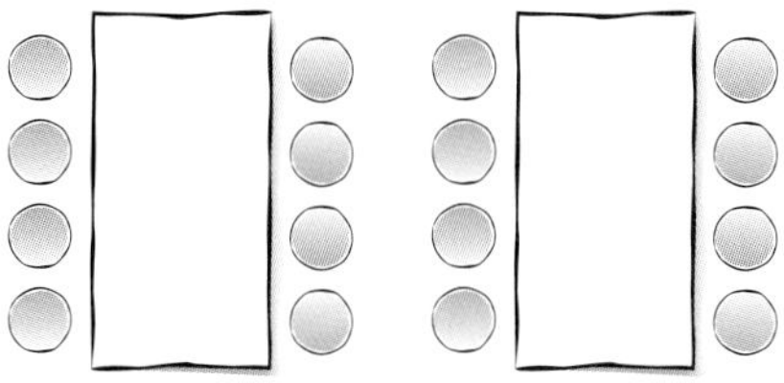

Arranging students by using two large tables will help maximize space in the classroom, but may also increase the likelihood of talking. The amount of noise generated would depend on the age and personalities of your students. Clear rules and expectations should be provided by the teacher to maintain a positive learning environment.

Student desks can be paired in rows in units of two. This formation is helpful in encouraging some communication, while limiting the number of students involved.

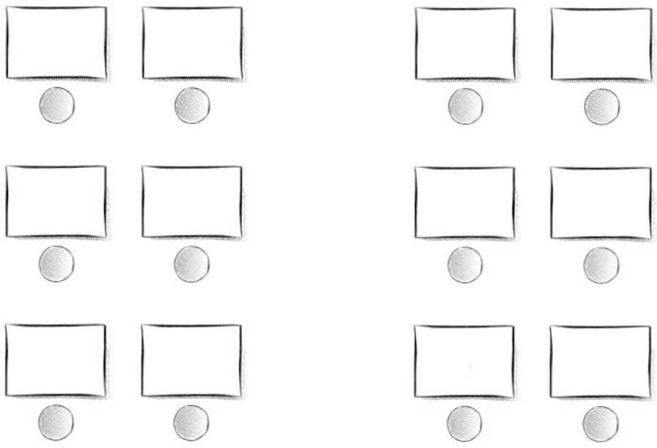

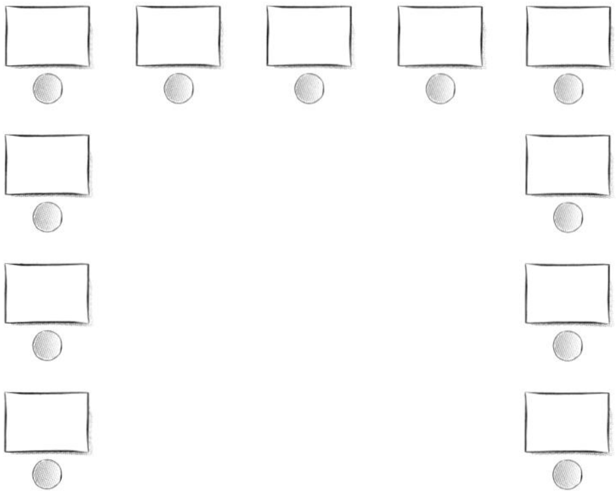

Student desks can be organized in a U shape. If you plan to do a lot of class discussions and whole group interaction, this is a good format. It can, however, be difficult for students who have a hard time staying on task. Not only are they surrounded by classmates, but they can see what everyone in the room is doing. This may be too much for the student who is easily distracted.

For a large class, student desks can be organized in two concentric U shapes. This is a useful design as a way of keeping everyone close to the teacher.

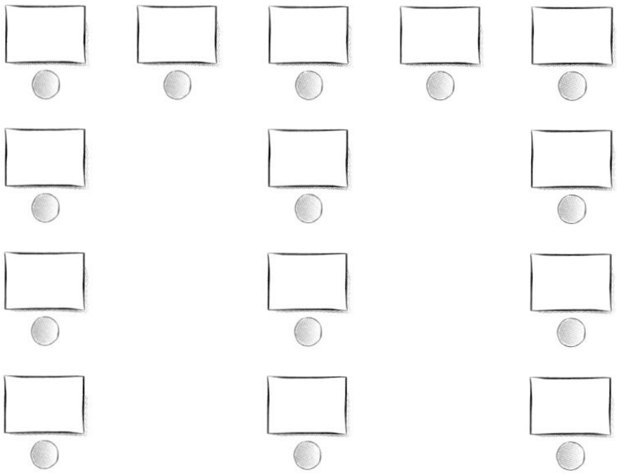

It is not necessary to keep student desks in the same formation all year. If you find that a certain arrangement is not working for you, change it. If you find one that works, keep it. Whatever desk formation you choose, change individual seating within the formation every two to four weeks to allow students to see new faces and hear new ideas. Students can take their desks with them to their new spot, or just take their belongings and place them in a new desk.

Teacher's Desk

The teacher's desk should be placed in a way that best helps you function efficiently in the classroom. If you plan to sit at your desk and interact with students, then place your desk where you have the best view. Many teachers place their desk at the side or the back of the room. This placement reflects the teacher's role as a guide who participates in learning, rather than one who directs. The placement of the teacher's desk will either invite student access or limit it. It is not necessary to allow student access to your desk in order to be a friendly and open teacher.

Bulletin Boards

 Bulletin boards are one of the most visible items in the room. Avoid crowded or cluttered bulletin boards because they can be intimidating and are often overlooked. They do not convey the sense of a well-organized teacher.

 Avoid leaving a bulletin board blank, unless you or the children are in the process of designing it. If you have nothing to display, cover it with bright wrapping paper and display student work or student photographs.

 Decide whether you want bulletin boards to be permanent or changed periodically. If you have several boards, you may want some to change and some to stay the same. The permanent ones can be in the less accessible places.

Bulletin boards can be covered with a variety of materials such as butcher paper, wrapping paper, or wallpaper. Cloth also makes a nice backing for bulletin boards and can be stapled into place, just like paper. If you plan to leave the covering on between board changes, use something that will wear well. A nonseasonal color is best if you plan to leave it on a long time.

Borders used on a bulletin board can make it look more finished. Borders can be purchased or handcrafted by you or your students using narrow strips of butcher paper. If you use a seasonal border, be sure to change it when the season ends.

The shape of the board need not confine you. You can hang large sheets of covering to drape, extend, and reshape the edges of the board.

Carefully choose colors when planning a bulletin board. Use calming colors whenever possible. Be careful of bright, bold colors. Vibrant colors tend to agitate young children. Try using cool colors to create a peaceful mood. Avoid placing large portions of primary colors on primary colors.

Words and messages should contrast from the rest of the bulletin board. Letter size should be large enough to view from across the room.

If you want students to design or assemble a bulletin board, be sure the canvas is easily accessible. Avoid having students stand on a chair or stool to reach the top of the board.

Student work can be displayed on bulletin boards and changed as subjects expand. Be sure each student's name can be seen on the displayed work. A time-saving step is to create reusable nameplates out of white index cards to hang near students' work. Laminate them for durability.

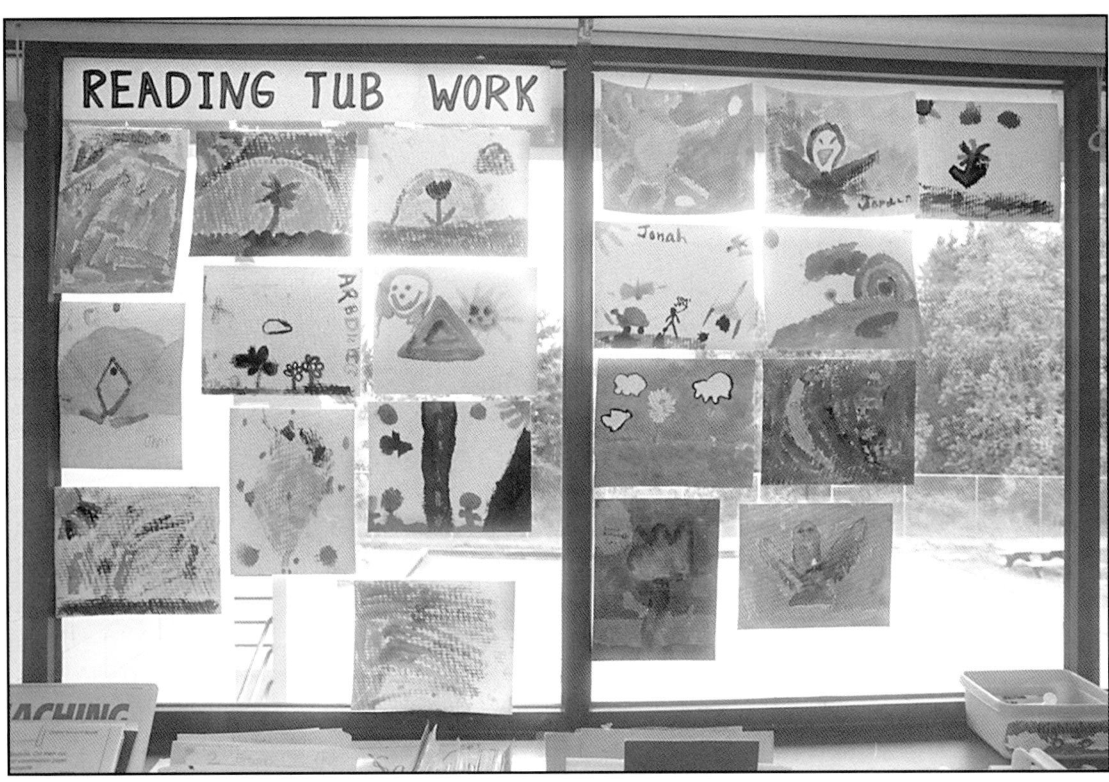

 When displaying student work on a long-term basis, it's best to follow a specific format. For example, you may choose to spotlight students' writing, their best work of the week, or artwork. For a long-term display, each student should have his or her own spot. This will make student work easier to find—for them and for you. Attach their work to the bulletin board with pushpins; this provides a way to add future papers. Punch holes in the upper corners of the work (you may have to punch several overlapping holes), then slip the hole over the pushpin. This enables you to store the displayed work on the bulletin board throughout the year by adding each new piece to the top. At the end of the year, you have a ready-made packet of work to send home.

 If you plan to reuse a bulletin board display in the future, store all its pieces together in a large resealable bag. Letters, pictures, and borders can all be stored together to avoid having to reassemble the next time you use the display.

 Your bulletin boards should reflect the high-quality standards you require of your students. Correct spelling and neatness are a must.

Creating Board Space

If you find yourself in a classroom without display space, use materials to cover the walls to create the illusion of bulletin boards.

 Display student work on doors and windows. First, cover space with butcher paper, then frame using borders.

 Tack, tape, or pin paper directly to walls.

 Mount corkboard, purchased in bulk at a hardware supply store, to the walls.

 Attach lightweight rugs to the wall to create a warm and cozy feeling.

Whiteboards and Chalkboards

Whiteboards and chalkboards are important messengers of information. Be sure to keep them clean and uncluttered. Clean the board and ledge as often as necessary to avoid streaks and an accumulation of chalk or marker dust. Be cautious of children who may have dust allergies. When erasing a large area, use two erasers. Hold one in each hand and do a windshield wiper movement. This will make a tedious task more fun while amusing your students at the same time.

If you write your daily schedule on the board, always write it in the same spot each day. This will help children get into the habit of checking for information.

To record names of students who have missing homework or overdue library books, and to display other notices, create a "business box." Use colored tape or a paper border to create a square on the chalkboard or whiteboard. The information can then be written in the "business box." Students will get in the habit of checking for their names.

Don't use your board to stick up a lot of reminder notes. This will make the space look very busy, and for some children it will be distracting. A selected number of reminder notes can be used. Place reminders next to subject areas, such as bus notes near the exit, lunch notes near the lunch lineup area, and private notes in your private file.

Books and Bookshelves

The generous presence and easy availability of colorful and attractive books in the classroom will encourage children to read. Design a comfortable reading area near the books where students can relax and enjoy reading. A small rug or individual carpet square can define a reading area. An appliance box, beanbag chair, or even a canoe lined with pillows make a cozy reading nook.

All books should be clearly labeled with your name or the school name and room number. Whenever possible, identification should be in the same spot in every book.

Students must have a clear understanding of your expectations for the care and handling of books. Any book that is torn or soiled should be reported to you so it can be repaired, replaced, or taken out of circulation. Circulating books that are in poor condition decreases a child's respect for them.

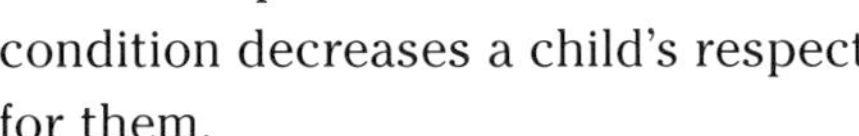

Permit students to check out some of the classroom books to take home. Place each book in a large resealable bag with a library check-out card. Students sign the card, leave it in the appointed spot, and take the book home in the resealable bag.

One book for one night is a good policy for young children.

Letting children take home a book of their choice helps encourage them to read independently. Although this practice may increase the risk of losing a few books to damage or misplacement, it is well worth the risk.

Use a magazine or book display rack to encourage students to read. Display covers whenever possible as they are specifically designed to excite a child's interest. Standing books on top of a low bookshelf is a good way to show off book covers.

Display books in some meaningful order rather than putting them out randomly. Group them according to topic, size, or type of book, such as magazine, hardback, or paperback. This helps students focus on what they are looking for and also sends the message that books are valuable and worth caring for.

If no shelves are available, several wide-mouthed plastic baskets can be used to group books together. This kind of storage also permits you to arrange the books so that many covers are visible.

Offer books written in a variety of reading levels and on many different topics.

Periodically rotate books, storing out-of-circulation materials in the cupboard for a few weeks. Next time you bring them out, they'll be seen with fresh eyes.

No matter what level students you have, it's important to have as many reference books as you can beg, borrow, or buy. Include dictionaries, atlases, encyclopedias, thesauruses, and how-to books.

Let students see you reading and using books. Many schools designate a specific time for sustained reading each day. Model the joy of reading by reading yourself. If your school doesn't have a school-wide sustained reading period, introduce one to your class. Reading aloud for 15 minutes a day motivates students to read on their own.

Books that students do not need access to can be placed out of the central classroom area, such as inside cupboards or on high shelves. Place your own reference books near your desk, with those you use most at eye level.

Have a selection of books available for parents. Include educational magazines, parenting books, and materials that address child development. Also include books parents might enjoy reading to their children. To keep track of the books, have a readily visible sign-out sheet with spaces for parents to write their names, book titles, and the date.

Bookshelves can be used as dividers to create different areas within the classroom. Be sure students are still visible to you—no matter where they are in the room. Low bookshelves work best as dividers—they don't block your view, and there is less risk of them accidentally toppling over.

If a bookshelf is too tall for your students, consider removing the shelves and turning the bookshelf on its side. Place books in crates and baskets.

If you live in an earthquake area, bookcases must be carefully bolted to the wall.

Cupboards and Storage Space

Plan your use of cupboard and storage space carefully. These spaces can be helpful to you and should not be seen as just a place to stash unwanted items.

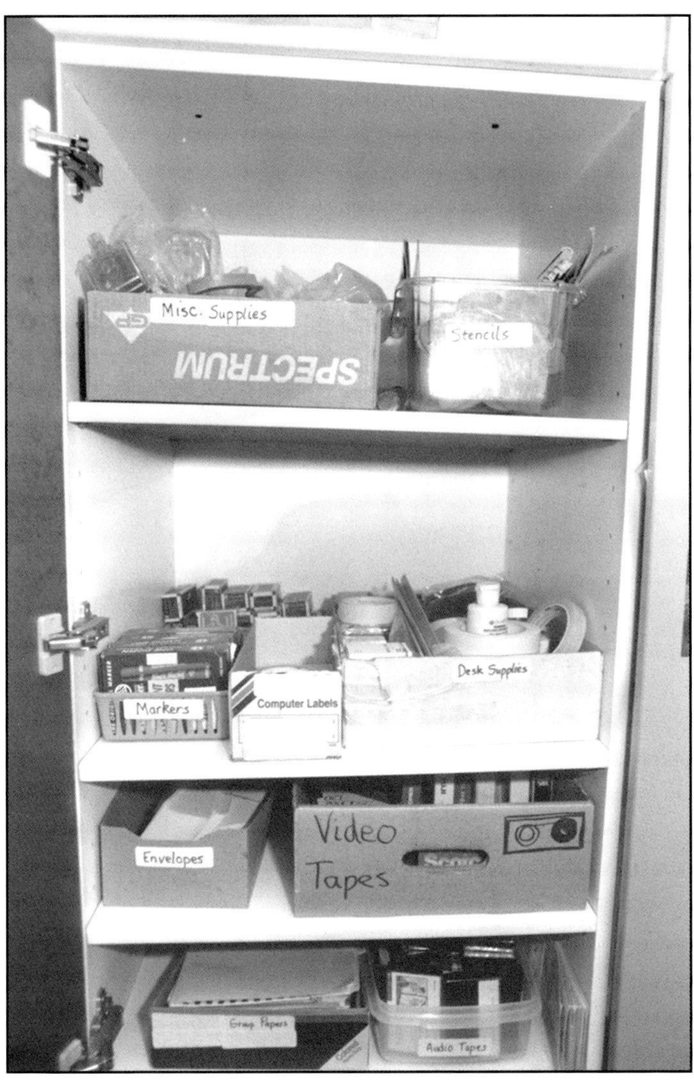

First, draw out a storage plan to visualize your ideas. This makes it easy to make changes and will save moving things twice.

Anything you don't have to store, don't. Donate, dump, or deliver it to someone who wants it, needs it, or has room for it.

Keep a box in one of your cupboards labeled "Miscellaneous Items." This will save you from fretting over where to put small items that seem to have no specific home.

Have a "Transition Box" for items that you think you may want to discard, but are not quite sure yet. Leave the items in the box until you are sure you will not need them. Often the items in the box lose their importance and can be happily discarded.

Anything that looks cluttered should be stored behind doors to avoid visual overload. Label cupboards on the outside or on the edge of the shelf. You may think you will remember how you have organized them, but you may not. For storage areas that children will be accessing, the labels should be on the outside of the cupboard in large and clearly understood letters. This will cut down on rummaging.

Whenever possible, store items near where you will need them. Use high or out-of-reach cupboards for materials students do not need access to.

Try to place related items together. This will save you time when you are putting together projects and activities.

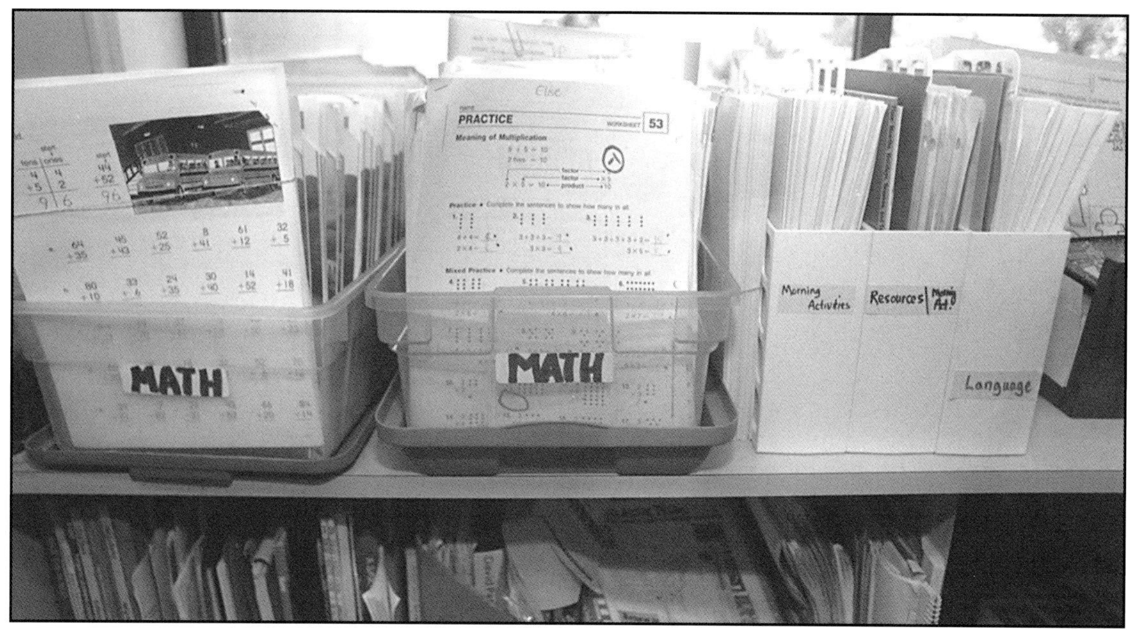

If you live in an earthquake area, be careful of how you fill cupboards. Heavy items on high shelves can be dangerous. If your school doesn't provide door latches, place a stick or child-safety latch through the handles to prevent doors from opening.

Use tall cupboard spaces, such as those designed for hanging coats, to store large posters. (Although many classrooms provide large shallow drawers for such posters, piling them one on top of the other makes them very impractical to use. Such a stack becomes too heavy to sort through.) In the tall closet, stand the posters on end and use pieces of tagboard as dividers. Label the outer edge of the tagboard with a computer address label folded lengthwise and attach it to the front and back for double visibility.

If you are short on storage space, use large plastic tubs available at variety and hardware stores. Tubs can be stacked in a corner and labeled for easy access. Do not mix items. Each tub should contain only related items. Tubs can be given a general subject label such as "Math," or a more specific title such as "Place Value." Be specific—in the long run it will save you time.

Classroom Supplies

Post a reproducible shopping list inside a cupboard. As supplies run out and new items are needed, simply check off the depleted items. As needs expand, add new items to the list. Before purchasing supplies, check to see if items are available through the district.

CHAPTER TWO

Organizing Routines and Rituals

"Routines and rituals" are the many activities that are done day after day and week after week in your classroom. They're not the interesting units and creative lessons that you teach your students. They're not the beautiful works of art or unique sculptures that your students share on parent night. Rather, routines and rituals are the nuts and bolts of classroom life. They include attendance, where to store coats, lining up, recess equipment, lunches, sharing, classroom helpers, fire drills, assemblies, bathroom use, daily schedules, field trips, and classroom management in general.

Attendance

Most schools require the classroom teacher to take attendance each day. The obvious goal of taking attendance is to record, for both the office and parents, who is absent. Also, state funding is often tied in to student attendance. The less obvious, yet more important, goal of taking attendance is to purposefully validate each student's presence in your classroom. Students need to know that you are aware of them and pleased that they are present.

Taking attendance should not be a time-consuming task. It should take no more than five to seven minutes. Any more than this and it becomes a waste of time. If you find that your attendance-taking routine is taking more time than it should, consider changing it.

Depending on the age of your students, there are many ways attendance can be taken. You can make this a learning activity that involves the whole class or a quick check that involves just a few people. For older students, a quick check may be all the time you have. Try to involve the whole class if you have young students. Taking role offers an opportunity to practice listening skills.

 Read names from the attendance sheet out loud and have students stand when they hear their names.

 Read names from the attendance sheet by saying, "Good morning Josh," "Good morning Lindsay," etc. Have students reply by saying good morning back to you.

 Read names from the attendance sheet out loud and have students respond with a certain word relating to a classroom activity. For example, if you have been studying nouns, students could respond with a noun when they hear their names. Following a unit on food groups, students could respond with an item from a particular food group when their names are read.

 Read names from the attendance sheet out loud and have students turn in homework when their names are read.

There are many ways of taking student attendance without involving the whole class. One way is to write each student's name on a plastic milk bottle cap and glue a magnet to the back of it. Place the magnetic caps on the chalkboard or whiteboard near the ledge. Draw a smiley face on the board above where the magnets are to be placed. As students arrive at school, have them move their magnet up to the smiley face. You can quickly see who is absent by noticing which magnets remain at the ledge. Be sure to do a quick check to see if students are really absent or have just forgotten to move their magnets.

Have a student read the names from the attendance sheet out loud and have students stand when they hear their names. Allow different students to be in charge of reading the names every day.

Another way is to hang a clothesline in the classroom. Write students' names on clothespins. As students come in, have them remove their names from the clothesline and drop them into a nearby basket labeled "Attendance" or "I'm Here." The clothespins of absent students will remain on the clothesline. At the end of the school day, replace clothespins for the next day. The clothesline must be low enough for students to reach, but should not be placed where they're apt to walk into it.

Have a hat with a large brim turned upside down near the classroom door. Attach clothespins (label each pin with a student's name) around the hat brim. As students walk into the classroom have them remove their clothespins and drop them into the bowl of the hat.

For a student-made element, give each student a 4" × 2" (10 cm × 5 cm) piece of tagboard. Using the tagboard, have them create self-portraits, from head to toe. Put out two baskets—one labeled, "Home," and the other labeled, "School." Place all student tagboard portraits in the "Home" basket. As students enter the classroom, have them place their portraits in the "School" basket.

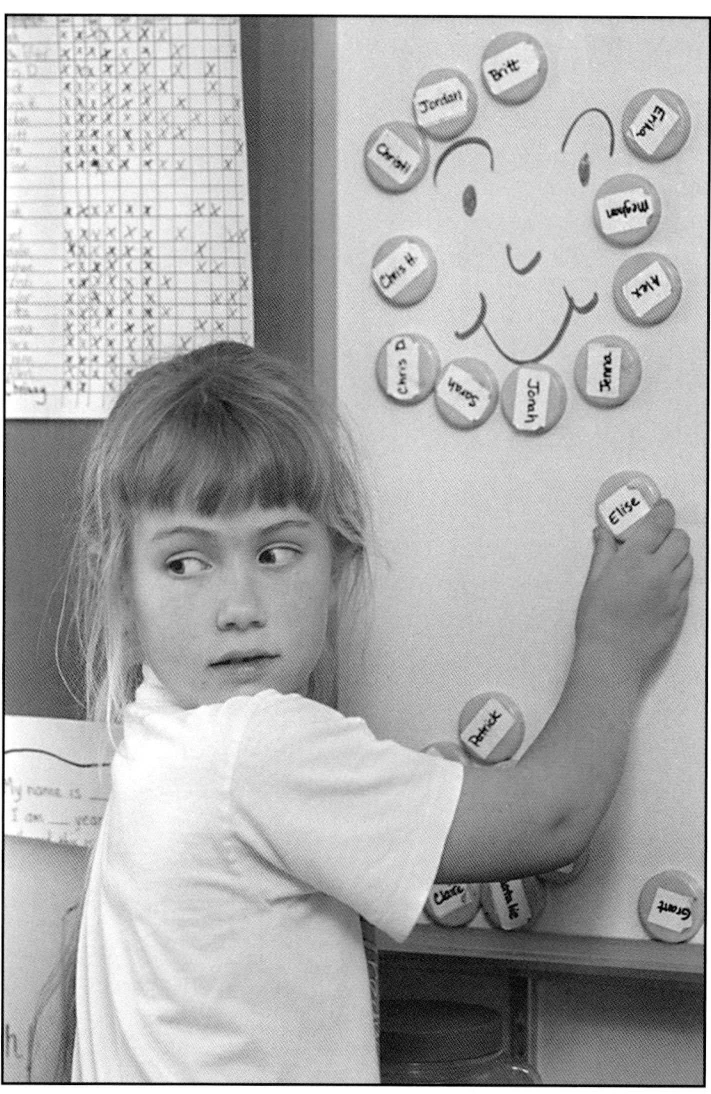

Coats and Backpacks

Your classroom may or may not have coat hooks for students to use. If your classroom does have them, don't feel obligated to use them if they aren't convenient. Coats can be kept on the back of student chairs. This makes them handy for recess or emergency drill purposes. The shoulders of the coats should be hung over the chair back. If the chair back has a space in it, loop the sleeves around the chair frame. This keeps coats from hanging on the floor. If lice is a problem in your area be sure coats are not hung together. Lice will spread quickly.

Consider using coat hooks for backpacks. Have students get into the routine of hanging backpacks up as soon as they walk into class. Homework and other items that need to be turned in should be removed from the packs prior to the day's first lesson to avoid unnecessary disruption.

Lining Up

Early in the school year, state the purpose of proper line behavior and explain exactly what your expectations are. Help students recognize the importance of being able to move efficiently through the school from one place to another. State clearly what you expect from your students when they are in line. Having an easy-to-remember checklist may help them get ready quickly. When possible, give choices. For example, hands may be in one of three places—clasped in front, at their sides, or clasped in back.

Depending on your students' age, they may need to practice walking in line. Allow time to accomplish this early in the year.

Do not allow your students to adopt a casual attitude toward line behavior. Explain that line etiquette is important in case of an emergency. It's sometimes thought that a casual, talkative line represents a high level of friendship and rapport between students and the teacher. In actuality, it represents a lack of manners and respect and can be annoying to those around you. In order to convince your students that you will follow up on your pre-set expectations for in-line behavior, wait until your line is completely quiet before leaving the classroom. At the beginning of the year you may have to allow extra time for this waiting period while students learn to be quiet.

Praise your students often for their orderly line behavior. By pointing out the rules that were followed, you are reinforcing good behavior.

If your students are walking in line and become disruptive, stop and wait for them to refocus. Encourage students to remind each other to be quiet by silently putting their index fingers across their lips.

If possible, alternate where you walk in line with your students. For younger students you may find it necessary to walk in front of the line most of the time, but fall back occasionally to be near the middle of the line. With older students, you can walk in the back of the line. This gives you a different perspective and it allows students to feel that you are confident of their abilities.

You may include the job of line leader in your classroom job list. The line leader should be at the head of the line whenever your class lines up. It is the student's responsibility to be a quiet leader and set a good example. If line leaders do not fulfill their duties, they should be relieved of their job temporarily. Offer them another chance later in the day.

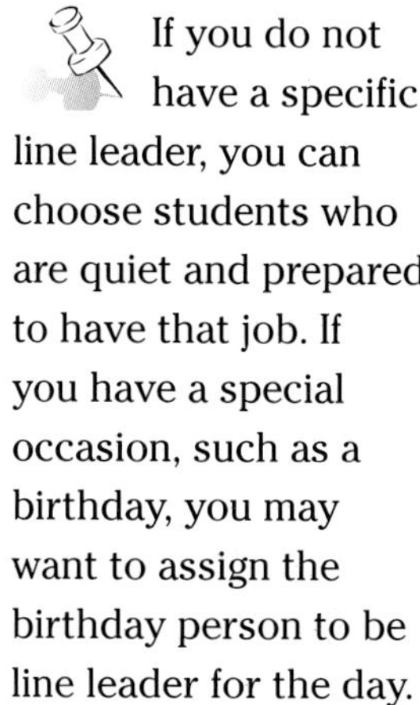

If you do not have a specific line leader, you can choose students who are quiet and prepared to have that job. If you have a special occasion, such as a birthday, you may want to assign the birthday person to be line leader for the day.

Some districts don't allow boys and girls to be segregated in different lines. Be aware of district guidelines and follow them, regardless of your personal preference.

Recess Equipment

If you keep recess equipment in your classroom, provide one particular area where it's always stored. A large box or tub is ideal for this purpose. Use a permanent marker to label recess equipment, writing your room number in several spots.

Have students be responsible for keeping track of recess equipment. If a student takes an item out to recess, it is his or her responsibility to bring it back to the classroom. Stating this policy is generally all you'll need for students to be responsible for the equipment. However, if equipment begins to disappear, you'll have to create a formal check-out system. Be warned that such systems can be time-consuming and laborious and should be avoided, if at all possible.

To create a formal recess equipment check-out system you'll need a clipboard, a check-out paper, and a pencil or pen attached to the clipboard with a string. Your check-out paper should list every item available for recess check-out. These items can be listed down the left margin. Next to each item should be two squares. The first square is for students to write their initials in when taking a piece of recess equipment. The second square is for students to write their initials in when the equipment is returned.

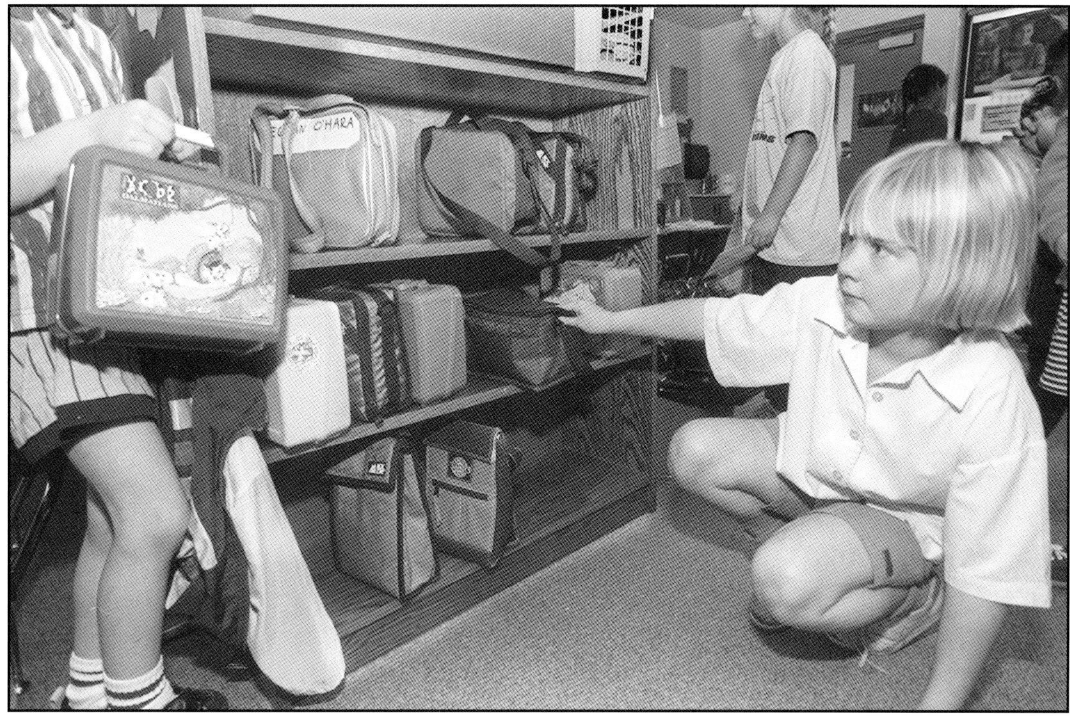

Lunches

Have students remove lunch boxes and bags from their backpacks upon arrival, so that any leaks or spills will be discovered early.

Keep a roll of absorbent paper towels on hand in case a lunchbox leak is discovered. Have students open their lunchboxes in the class sink and remove any wet or leaking items. If you don't have a class sink, keep a dish-washing tub handy for lunchbox cleanup. Store the paper-towel roll in the tub and tuck them away until both are needed.

Make sure all lunchboxes and bags are clearly labeled with first and last names. Lunches can be placed on a shelf or counter. Don't store them in a sunny spot where boxes will warm up and cause food to spoil.

Another idea is to directly place lunches in a laundry basket. At lunchtime, have monitors carry the distinctively-labeled basket to the lunch area. At the end of the lunch period, children will place their bags and boxes in the basket, and the lunch monitors will bring it back to class. If lunch cards need to be passed out, have a volunteer (depending on the age of your students) pass them out each day.

Use a wall chart with pockets to store lunch cards so students can be responsible for their own cards. Number the cards so they can be found easily and you can tell if some are missing. Lunch cards can also be stored in students' cubbyholes or mailboxes.

When numbering lunch cards have each student learn and remember his or her own number. Write students' numbers on their name tags to help them remember. Store the cards in numerical order, assigning a student the task of sequencing numbers.

Play an alphabet game while passing out lunch cards. Start with any letter in the alphabet and have students whose names (first or last) start with that letter stand up to receive their cards. Then have students whose names begin with the next letter in the alphabet stand and retrieve their card, and so on.

Streamline lunch procedures as much as you can so your students will know the routine. This will especially help on hectic days. Your students will know what to expect and will be able to work quickly.

Sharing

Most students—no matter what their ages—enjoy being in the spotlight, if only for a few moments. If your schedule allows, have sharing time each day. Decide if you want to encourage spontaneous sharing or just one share day per child each week. During sharing, have the student who will be sharing sit in front of the class on a stool or chair. Require that all other students listen attentively. This is an important skill for students to practice and it helps build positive interpersonal relationships. When the student who is sharing finishes, have him or her ask the class for any questions or comments. Consider writing on cue cards three standard prompt questions, utilizing several of the five *who, what, when, why,* and *where* inquiries.

If the student sharing is feeling shy or embarrassed about being in front of the class, he or she may need your initial support. To ease nerves, ask the student a few easy questions. Sometimes just standing next to a child can be a confidence booster.

Make sharing optional. Students should not be forced to share. Often, students can be encouraged and convinced to share, but if not, they should be allowed to listen to others. Some students may be slow to start sharing and may need your verbal assistance. Your dialogue may go something like this:

Teacher: *"What do you have to share today?"*

Student: *"A bunny."*

Teacher: *"Is your bunny real?"*

Student: *"No."*

Teacher: *"Does your bunny have a name?"*

Student: *"I don't know. Fuzzy, I think."*

Teacher: *"Where did you get your bunny?"*

Student: *"From my grandma."*

Teacher: *"Do you have anything else you want to tell us?"*

Student: *"No."*

Don't be discouraged by these kinds of interactions. Students benefit from sharing in front of others, no matter what form it takes. As they continue to share, their comfort level will grow and you'll be able to take a smaller role in their sharing.

You may have some students who love to share. They may claim the stage and ramble as long as they're allowed. For this student, sharing time can be an opportunity to practice focusing on one point and sticking to the topic. You may need to gracefully enforce a time limit. The following comments can be used to wrap up this student's sharing:

- *"Tell us one more thing, and then we will have questions."*
- *"What a wonderful story. Thanks for sharing it."*
- *"Your time is up, if you want to leave time for questions."*

Establish a "museum" in your classroom to display shared items. The museum can be a tub, box lid, or spot on a table. Make a portable museum by writing *museum* on a large piece of tagboard and placing it on top of a table or counter. Allow students to place their shared items in the museum for the day. Students should tell the class whether the object is for "touching" or "just looking at with your eyes" before placing it in the museum.

Discuss with your students the kind of items that may not be shared. Items not permissible would include anything not allowed at school, such as violent, gross, highly valuable, and breakable materials.

Students can be encouraged to bring in items that go along with classroom topics. Some possibilities include:

- Items of a particular color
- Items that begin with a certain letter
- Common nouns
- Transportation
- Student-crafted items
- Personally historic things, such as baby items
- Items from foreign countries
- Items with moving parts
- Items made from certain materials such as cotton or plastic.

If students want to share a pet or person be sure to have them check with you beforehand. Inquire about possible student allergies before allowing a pet to visit. If students touch the animal, be sure to have moist hand wipes available for hand-cleaning.

When students are finished sharing, encourage them to ask the class if there are any questions or comments. Allow only two questions or comments from the class.

Classroom Helpers

Using student helpers is a great way to involve everyone in the responsibilities of classroom life. Students love being helpers and generally take the job very seriously.

Classroom helpers need to reflect your management style. Decide which jobs you want students to do and which jobs you prefer to do yourself. This will vary depending on the age of your students. Some job possibilities include:

JOB	DESCRIPTION
Paper passer	passes out papers to students
Messenger	carries paperwork to office
Color guard	leads class in flag salute
Inspector	checks on classroom clean up
Line leader	leads line in and out of class
Recess monitor	checks to make sure equipment is returned
Light monitor	turns out lights when class leaves
Librarian	straightens classroom books
Attendance taker	takes attendance each morning
Lunch/drink monitor	retrieves lunchboxes from lunchroom

To simplify classroom organization, choose five to six jobs to assign to students. Some jobs can be a combination of tasks. For example, the inspector, librarian, or attendance taker can also be assigned to pick up the lunchboxes from the lunch room each day. Having a small number of jobs makes it easier to monitor the monitors. Selecting students to do various classroom jobs can be done in a variety of ways.

Post a "Helpers' Chart." The chart can have pictures illustrating each job, or it can have the name of the job, or both. Use job names that indicate what the job involves. For example, *paper passer, color guard,* or *line leader.* Helpers can be chosen weekly or daily depending on your particular class needs. If done weekly, choose helpers first thing Monday morning so they can begin their jobs right away. Daily helpers should be selected early in the morning or even the day before. Be sure students are clear about what each job involves. Student helpers from the week before can assist the new helpers if necessary.

One way of selecting student helpers is to have each student make a "helping hand" by tracing the outline of a hand onto a piece of construction paper and writing his or her name in the center. Decorate as desired and laminate for durability. Store the hands in a box or envelope labeled "Future Helpers." Each week, choose your helpers' hands and write the corresponding names on the chart. At the end of the week, move the hands to a box labeled "Past Helpers," and choose again. Keep a master record of student helpers and their jobs, disbursing tasks equitably.

Another way to choose helpers is to write each student's name on a clothespin. Choose one clothespin for each weekly job. Write the helpers that have been selected on the chart for the week.

Students can also be assigned a number. Write the numbers on a piece of paper or a plastic bottle cap. Place the numbers in a bowl or box. Select numbers to choose student helpers. Once a number has been selected, place it in a separate bowl so that all students have a chance to be helpers before you start over again.

Emergency Drills

Most schools do monthly emergency drills. Some schools inform teachers about upcoming drills. Before the first drill make sure you know which exit you're supposed to use and where you're supposed to take your students. Rehearse the drill prior to the first schoolwide practice evacuation.

Early in the school year, clearly explain the rules and expectations for student behavior in an emergency situation such as a fire drill, earthquake drill, or other required evacuation. Students must walk in an orderly way out of the building according to your directions.

Verify district policy regarding removal of personal items during emergency drills. If it's cold outside, and not against district policy, have students grab their coats from the backs of their chairs. Students should walk in single file with their hands to themselves unless you have instructed them otherwise. Require that students be attentive and quiet from the time you line up to leave the building until you re-enter the building after clearance. This "quiet" is important so that students can hear directions and instructions during the drill.

Show your students where the fire alarms in the building are located and explain how they work. Be sure your students know that pulling a fire alarm when there is not a fire or a suspected fire is against the law.

The emergency bell may be extremely loud and startle you and your students. Discuss the volume of the signal to prepare them for the loud noise. Encourage students to share stories about fire alarms or other loud noises to quell possible fear. The alarm and drill experience may frighten young children. Be sensitive to their fears and try to calm them.

Many schools have different types of drills, depending on their location. Be sure to know the types of drills your school has and the corresponding signals. All drills should be treated as if they were a real emergency. Each drill, whether fire, tornado, or earthquake, should be planned for and practiced. Reassure students that, most likely, the drill is a practice, while continuing to require emergency behavior.

As students exit the room, quickly lead them to the prearranged line-up area. Be sure to visually check your line as you're walking out of the building to be sure everyone is following promptly. Once you get to your designated evacuation spot, immediately conduct a student count.

Keep a class list with names and phone numbers of all of your students, along with an evacuation map, near the door through which you'll exit. Grab the list on your way out the door. Include the following checklist or create one pertinent to your classroom:

- windows closed?
- lights off?
- student coats?
- emergency kits?
- doors closed?

Depending on the age of your students, consider assigning a certain student the job of closing the doors and windows and turning off lights before leaving the room. If you have numerous windows and doors, you might want to assign the job to a team of students. If your students aren't old enough to close windows and doors, you will have to do this yourself before leaving the room. Note: It's a good policy to keep windows and doors closed, unless it is absolutely necessary to have them open. In many areas, it is against the fire code to have doors open. Ask your school office about specific regulations.

Many schools provide each teacher with an emergency tub or bucket. These buckets usually contain bandages, first-aid supplies, large garbage bags, several emergency space blankets, moist towelettes, a pair of scissors, masking tape, toilet paper, plastic bags, and some hard candies. If your school does not provide a classroom kit, ask your parent group to provide supplies or funding for you to make your own. If you have to make your own kit, use a plastic bucket with a lid and handle to hold enough provisions for a two-day period. Remember, you have to carry the bucket, so don't make it too heavy.

More and more schools require that parents provide individual emergency kits for their children. These kits generally contain provisions for a two-day period. Kit items include: a space blanket, a flashlight with two batteries, a large garbage bag, two pop-top cans of tuna, two individual serving boxes of cereal, three granola bars, two candy bars, three juice boxes, two individual servings of fruit in a can, a spoon, a letter of encouragement from home, a family photo, emergency contacts, and medical information. All items can be stored in a large resealable bag clearly labeled with the student's name. Store individual bags in a large plastic garbage can with wheels. If possible, store the can outside your classroom during school hours for easy access in the event of an emergency.

Discuss fire drills and their purpose with your students. Explain that in case there's ever a real emergency, it's important to practice how to leave the building in an orderly fashion. Encourage students to share their ideas, providing ample time for questions.

After each fire drill, debrief with students. Compliment them on their appropriate behaviors and remind them if improvement is necessary. Give them time to discuss their reactions and feelings to the drill.

If possible and appropriate for your grade level, invite firefighters to visit the classroom. This gives students an opportunity to see firefighters close up and to ask questions. A field trip to a fire station can also be productive.

Assemblies

Many schools have school-wide assemblies throughout the year. Most assemblies are held in the campus' largest room, which may be a gym or cafeteria. Students are generally required to sit on the floor during an assembly. Explain your expectations and rules for assembly behavior before attending your first campus gathering. Assembly behavior should begin as soon as you leave your classroom and continue until the assembly is over and you've returned back to class. Students should be respectful and polite. Additional rules may vary depending on your school's requirements. If possible, explain in advance what the assembly is about. This will help students be more active listeners. Pose several questions for them to consider during the program. Discuss the answers when you return to class.

Listen attentively and monitor your students during the program. If it's necessary to discipline a child during the assembly, do it discreetly. Tell students ahead of time what motions or facial expressions you will use to give them information during the assembly. Some examples of useful facial expressions are: a frown to discourage talking, hands on ears to encourage listening, and folded arms to remind students to keep their hands to themselves.

Bathroom Use

Your students will undoubtedly need to go to the bathroom during the day. Recess and break times are good opportunities for this, but students are usually engaged in playing and do not see this as prime bathroom time. Decide how you will handle the bathroom issue in your classroom so that it is the least distracting.

One method is to use hall or bathroom passes to regulate the number of students leaving the classroom at the same time. A hall or bathroom pass also gives students permission to be out of the room without a teacher. Most teachers choose to place the passes near the door where students can access them without disrupting the class. Bathroom passes should be large enough so they will not be easily lost, soft enough so they won't hurt a child, and "noiseless" enough to not be distracting. A variety of objects can be used—a tennis ball attached to a string, a plastic baby toy, or a cardboard square. As you are picking your objects, keep in mind that you will probably need to replace passes throughout the year.

Having students carry a bathroom pass to the bathroom with them exposes the pass to all kinds of germs. To avoid this exposure, have a student place the bathroom pass on his or her desk while in the bathroom. This lets the teacher know where the student is, and the pass stays clean.

If you choose not to use passes, be sure to have some way for students to inform you that they are leaving the room. A hand signal can be used. This way a student can inform you that he or she has to go to the bathroom without distracting the class.

Another method is to have clothespins with each student's name on it stored near the door in a small container. Have a large tagboard "B" attached to the wall near the door. Leave the edges of the "B" unattached so clothespins can be clipped to the edge as a student leaves for the bathroom. The container holding the clothespins should be user friendly so it is easy to find names, as some students do not have a lot of extra time on the way to the bathroom. (Avoid using clothespins for too many different purposes, as this may be confusing to your students. Use clothespins for no more than one or two purposes, and choose alternative systems for the others.)

Another signal is having a student place a colored index card on his or her desk before leaving the room. This informs you that the student is in the bathroom. When he or she comes back from the bathroom, the card is removed by the student and replaced in the storage area. These cards can be stored in an envelope, or on the chalkboard ledge.

Encourage students to wash their hands after they go to the bathroom, demonstrating proper procedure. Hands should also be washed before they eat snacks or lunch. By having parents provide containers of moist towelettes you can avoid long lines at the sink. Towelettes can be pooled for class use. Store them near the sink and pass them out to students before snack or lunch. They're also handy to use on inevitable clothing stains.

If a student's bathroom use is excessive, talk to his or her parent or guardian. The child may have an undetected medical condition, or a reaction to stress.

If you have young students, keep a collection of spare clothes. These can be obtained from a local thrift store or parent donations. Have a range of sizes for both boys and girls. Allow students to borrow the clothes as necessary, placing their soiled clothes in a sealable plastic bag and sent home for parents to wash and return to school. Establish a zero tolerance policy for teasing of any kind, including bathroom accidents.

Daily Schedules

Daily schedules provide an overview of what the day holds. Schedules can be written directly on the board or they can be written on reusable cards. These cards can be made from sentence strips or tagboard. Write one daily activity on each card and then laminate the cards. They can then be placed in a store-bought sentence strip holder or taped directly to the board. A daily schedule might include the following such as the list on the right:

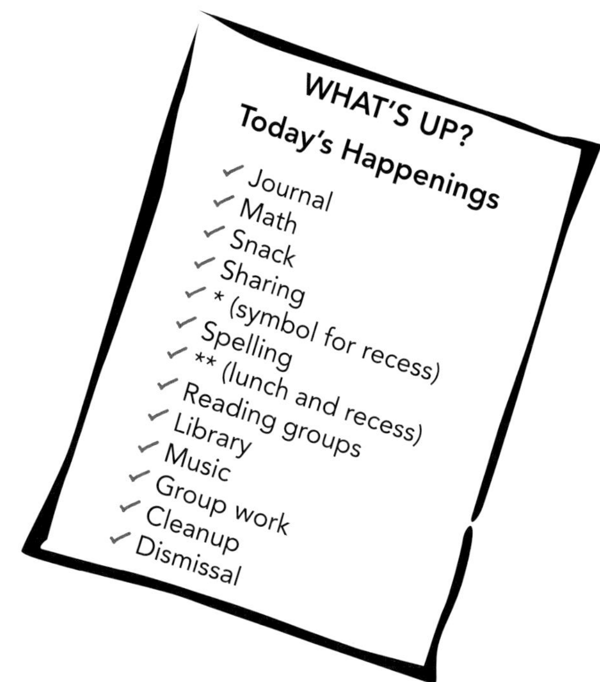

 Students like to know what their day will include. Post the day's schedule somewhere in the room. Use a heading for the schedule that reflects its importance. Options might include: "Our Daily Work," "Important News," "Priorities," "Now" (for work you will do today), and "Later" (for work that is coming up). If the daily schedule changes, be sure to inform students.

 If your students are too young to read independently, use pictures, along with the words, to illustrate the schedule.

 Even if your students do not appear to be referring to the schedule, continue to post it. In time, they'll come to rely upon it.

 Daily schedules can include the times activities will occur. There are both pros and cons for using times. For very young students, times may be distracting, while older students (second grade and older) may find them useful. Using time limits flexibility since students will keep track of the clock.

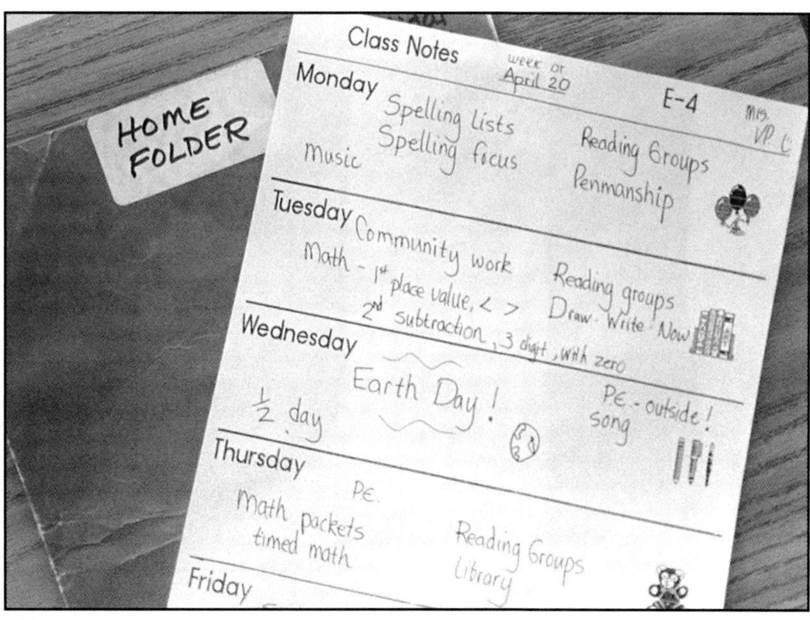

A daily schedule can also be more casual and include only highlights of the day. Using words like *now* and *later* or abbreviations like *a.m.* and *p.m.* can give your schedule a more general nature such as:

A.M.	**P.M.**
math, reading, spelling, snack	science, penmanship, music, computer

Use symbols for repetitive events like recess. An asterisk (*) can be used to represent short recesses, and two asterisks (**) can be used for longer recesses.

Field Trips

Field trips can be fabulous experiences for your students, but keeping forms and paperwork organized can be a challenge for the teacher. Keep in mind that you want things to go as smoothly as possible for everyone involved. This includes students, parents, bus drivers, school secretaries, business office secretaries, merchants, and anyone else involved in the field trip.

As you plan the trip, create a file folder of all the papers you accumulate. Write significant phone numbers on the front of the folder for easy access.

Use a large manila envelope to collect student permission slips and field-trip money. Write the name of each student who turns in a permission slip on the front of the envelope before placing the permission slip inside. If a student also brings in money for the trip, write a dollar symbol next to his or her name on the front of the envelope.

If volunteers are needed for the field trip, be sure to ask for parent helpers when you send home the field-trip announcement. Many parents and guardians work and will need to request time off, so send notes home well in advance of the trip.

If a student's parent volunteers to go on the field trip, mark a "V" next to his or her name on the front of the envelope. This will give you a quick view of how many parents you're expecting. If parents are required to pay a fee, place an additional dollar symbol next to the student's name and check it off once the parent has paid.

Be sure parents understand that it will be necessary for them to supervise not only their children, but other children as well. Each volunteer should be given a list of students they will supervise. An index card works well for this list. Keep a master list of parent/student matches.

If you are traveling a long distance, you may want to prepare lap boards for each student. Lap boards can be made by collecting math papers, puzzles, hidden pictures, scrambled sentences, and a variety of other worksheets that fit your students' ability level. Attach the papers inside a file folder by placing two or three staples at the top of the opened folder. Punch a hole in the folder and attach a pencil with a string. Make a pencil holder by cutting two ½" (1.25 cm) slits, 4" (10.2 cm) apart, in the top inside section of the folder in the style of a clipboard. Slip the pencil into the cutout sleeve. The file folder will provide a hard surface on which students can write, and will keep their pencil handy.

Be sure to carry some extra items with you on your field trip. A field trip checklist might include:

- extra pencils with erasers
- extra lap boards
- bandages
- list of parent helpers and students
- copy of permission slips
- name, address, and phone number of person at destination
- name, address, and phone number of person at school site
- first-aid kit

Respond promptly to a parent or guardian's offer to help. Communicate your needs by sending home a confirmation letter.

Behavior Management

In managing a classroom, your goal should be to create a safe environment for children and adults. Find a management style that works for you and reflects caring, sincerity, and respect. The most important word in classroom management is *respect.* Without it, you and your students cannot create a positive learning environment. Model it, teach it, nurture it, give it, and receive it.

Establish your expectations for classroom behavior beginning on the first day of school. Your expectations should include the use of good manners, a demonstration of courtesy, kindness, and tolerance.

Post classroom rules. Review and discuss classroom standards so that everyone knows what is expected. Rules might include information about bringing pencils, not chewing gum, and not running in the halls. Expectations for learning, such as the following, should also be included:

- *Be considerate of others*
- *Share your best self*
- *Be responsible for your own learning*
- *If you need help—ask!*

Many schools have standardized discipline policies. Be familiar with your school and district's specific policies. If your school does not have a standard policy, check with other teachers at your grade level to see what they they do. Find a plan that you believe in and can enforce without hesitation.

Once you've decided on a discipline plan, explain it to your students and parents. Be sure that you are clear and precise so that your expectations are understood. If you send home a written discipline policy, request that parents return a form that states they've read and understood the material.

A multistep discipline plan allows students to change their behavior along the way and avoid negative consequences. An example of a multistep plan might take the following form:

Step One:
Verbal warning about behavior

Step Two:
Name is written on the board

Step Three:
Check by name

Step Four:
Loss of privileges (recess, free time)

If the student changes the behavior after Step Two, erase his or her name from the board. If the behavior changes after Step Three, erase the check. If the student does not change his or her behavior after Step Four, it's time to phone home to explain the situation to a parent or guardian.

You may have some students who need constant reinforcement regarding their behavior. It may be necessary to develop a contract. A contract can be as simple as an index card taped to the student's desk. Each time an appropriate behavior is noticed, a sticker can be added to the card by the teacher. The student's goal is to earn a certain number of stickers to win a privilege such as, lunchtime with the teacher, extra free time, or a special activity. Send the card home at the end of the week for parents to review. Each week, start a new card.

For a simple management system, an "Oops Board" can be effective. When students forget what they should be doing, forget their manners, or forget how to be considerate of others, list their names on the board. Prior to putting their names on the board, give them fair warning.

- Once on the board, if a student changes his or her behavior, erase the name with no further consequences.

- If behavior doesn't change before recess or free time, he or she must forfeit a play time. Be sure to report this to parents, either by a quick phone call or a note home. Purchase a stamp with the word *Oops* on it and use it to stamp the student's daily calendar. This lets parents know that the student has lost a privilege because of unacceptable behavior.

Teaching students about feelings and how to handle them is an important aspect of a classroom management plan. Be sure your students know that it is all right to have feelings. We all feel angry, happy, sad, mad, tired, frustrated, excited, and so on. Students need to learn to manage those feelings. Consider posting the following thought-provoking reminder in your room:

It's OK to be mad.
It's not OK to be mean.

Provide your students with a list of the following problem-solving options:

- Give an "I" message (a message starting with the word *I*)
- Walk away
- Talk it over
- Ignore the behavior
- Do something else
- Ask for help

Encourage students to interact as a school family. Remind them that they will be spending a lot of time together. They have the opportunity to create an inspiring, productive, and significant relationship with their school family.

Provide students with an opportunity to discuss problems and concerns they have regarding behaviors. Keep a Worry Bee in your classroom. A Worry Bee can be made out of yellow and black construction paper and then laminated. Attach a magnet to the back so students can hang the Worry Bee on the board when they have a concern or worry. The Worry Bee is your cue to take time to hear a student's worry and discuss the problem as a class. To avoid tattling, inform students that they must have tried two problem-solving options before posting the Worry Bee.

The preceding pages describe a very simple behavior management plan. Problem-solving strategies and other behavior management topics are discussed in detail in the second half of this book.

CHAPTER THREE

Organizing Student Work

Throughout the year you will handle hundreds of pieces of paper. Most will be student work that eventually ends up in the teacher's file, parent's file, or on the student's desk. Ideally, papers of value should not end up in students' desks, as they are unlikely to emerge again. Keeping track of student work is an organizational challenge. To stay on top of it, you'll need to keep track of which work has been given out and to whom, which work has come in and from whom, and what level of mastery each student has achieved on each piece of work. By using efficient organizational strategies, you'll be able to meet these goals and manage the abundance of student work year after year.

Passing Out and Collecting Student Assignments

When passing out new student work, place a small number of papers at each table or row. Allow students to distribute papers to their row or table mates, and have the last student hold up any extra papers. This saves you from counting the exact number for each row and gives students a chance to be involved in the process. Require students to hold up extras quickly and quietly. Students soon catch on to this time-saving routine.

Choosing a student to be table or row organizer for a day or week is a good way to have a readily-available helper. Allow the organizer to be responsible for passing out papers to each row or table. Organizers should be changed often, offering every child an opportunity to help. Assignments students do every day should be placed in an easily accessible spot to encourage them to take responsibility for picking them up and completing them. Examples might include a daily activity that is completed every morning upon arrival, or an assignment that is completed each day after recess. Keep the spot the same so students will always know where to find the material.

Keep a container or basket in your classroom labeled, "Homeward Bound" in which you can place school notices that go home with students. As soon as these items are brought to your mailbox or classroom, place them in the basket. Check the basket before the end of each day so that information can be sent home.

When collecting student work to be corrected, use a colored, plastic, rectangular basket. Keep the basket in front of the room and have students place their finished work in the basket. Always refer to the basket by the same name such as "The Blue Basket." This helps students remember where to stack completed assignments.

You can create separate collection areas for different subjects, such as "Math in," "Spelling in," "Writing in." Clearly labeled dish-washing tubs make useful storage bins. If someone other than you, such as an aide or volunteer, corrects student work, write out specific directions for correcting. Laminate and store in the tub.

Have a "Ketchup Basket" for not-yet-completed student work. Encourage students to retrieve work and finish, as time permits. Decorate the basket with a real plastic ketchup bottle or pictures of ketchup bottles.

Consider collecting and displaying student work using a clothesline and clothespins. Use a marker to color the long, flat side of enough clothespins to have one for each student. As students turn in work, use colored clothespins to hang it. If more than one clothespin is needed for a particular piece, use one colored pin and one plain. A quick glance at the clothesline and the unused supply of colored pins will tell you how many students have not turned in their work.

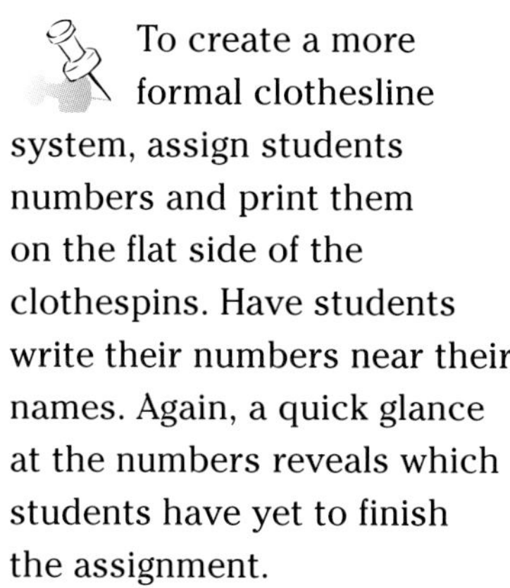

To create a more formal clothesline system, assign students numbers and print them on the flat side of the clothespins. Have students write their numbers near their names. Again, a quick glance at the numbers reveals which students have yet to finish the assignment.

Keep a basket in the classroom labeled "Friday Boxes." All the papers that are completed and corrected during the week can be placed in the basket. On Fridays, distribute papers to students' cubby-holes, slots, or file folders. Papers that have no names should be left in the "Friday Boxes" basket to be claimed later. On Friday, have students take their work home.

To give your class an added opportunity to practice listening skills, tell students that they are going to arrange their papers from the "Friday Boxes" into a specific order. Students should place their pile of papers on one side of their desks, leaving an area clear to start a new pile. Use one student's stacks of papers to demonstrate paper order. Hold up one paper at a time for the class to see. Instruct students to find the corresponding paper, hold it up, then place it in their stacks. Sorting through papers this way gives students a chance to claim any unnamed papers left in the "Friday Boxes." While students are arranging papers, have them check to make sure they don't have another student's paper. Staple each pile and send it home for parents to review.

Work to Be Saved or Shared

Throughout the year you may want to save samples of student work to send home or pass on to next year's teacher to show student progress. This work can be saved in a variety of portfolio systems:

One way to create a student portfolio is to give each student a large manila envelope labeled with his or her name. Every day allow students to add completed and corrected work they want to save. This "Treasure Envelope" will encourage them to take pride in their work. Send the envelopes home once every two weeks to be shared with parents. After viewing the work, parents and students can decide together which work should remain in the "Treasure Envelope." The envelope is then returned to school. Continue this process throughout the year.

Another way to create student portfolios is to have student file folders. These files can be stored in a file cabinet or desk drawer. At the end of the year, mount each piece of student work on construction paper and bind the papers together with staples, yarn, or spiral spines. This becomes a memory packet of the year's work for each student to take home.

Student work can also be collected by using large manila envelopes labeled for each month of the school year. Every month choose one or two assignments per child to place in the envelope, making sure names are on them. At the end of the year, collate student papers, then staple or bind them into a packet ready to take home.

Students can be included in selecting work that they'd like to have in their portfolios. Collect work throughout the year that represents a variety of skills and mastery. Store these, and at the end of the year have students sort through their work, selecting items they'd like to put into their portfolios. Suggest criteria for saveable items. Students should look for work that represents their progress and effort. Mount or otherwise package material for students to take home. Depending on the age of your students and the needs and requirements of your district, you may need to develop a more complex portfolio system. There are many books, articles, and web sites covering this topic.

To encourage students to share their work and compliment the work of others, keep a box in which students can place work they'd like to share with the class. This work might include drawings, tests, or written assignments. Designate a specific day and time for group sharing. Make positive comments and ask, "How was it done?"

Create a "Proud Work" binder using plastic page protectors (available at office or variety stores). In the lower left-hand corner of each page protector, write a student's name. Students can then place work in the binder that they would like to share with the class. Invite them to add work each week. Before work goes into the binder, it should be teacher-corrected. Keep the binder in the reading area or another accessible spot. The page protectors can then be sent home at the end of the year with each student.

Giving Feedback on Student Work

Celebrate the work your students do. Let them know that their work is not only important to you, but also to their parents. The more immediate the feedback, the more productive it becomes. Use a variety of methods for complimenting work. Students of all ages enjoy stickers, stamps, and personal notes. Vary your use of these items.

Keep a sticker basket in your classroom. Allow students to place stickers on their completed and corrected work. Determine your criteria for sticker use.

Create a work slip to send home with work that was not completed at school and needs to be done at home. Make a work slip using a half sheet of paper and include the following information: student's name, date, work to be completed, and date to be returned. Keep blank forms on hand.

Explain to students that a work slip does not mean the student is being punished or penalized. Work slips merely provide parents with information regarding what is expected by the teacher.

In order to be sure parents see the work, ask them to sign the papers and have their children return them to school.

Provide some kind of feedback on all student work. Feedback may be as simple as a smiley face indicating that the work has been seen. More detailed feedback may involve a phrase or note written specifically to each student. Adjust your feedback according to the depth and complexity of the assignment, but it is important that children know you have taken the time to look over their work.

When students neglect to return their homework it's important to keep parents informed. One way to do this is to send a notice to parents that requests a specific assignment be completed by the student.

CHAPTER FOUR

Organizing Communication

The ability to communicate with students, parents, and staff may well be the most critical element in achieving success as a teacher. Effective communication is vital to the creation of positive rapport with colleagues. Communication skills are an essential foundation on which professional success is founded.

In written communication, our message is colored by the words we choose, the clarity of our thoughts, appearance, and neatness, and overall appropriateness.

In oral communication, far more is involved. We send out messages through body posture, hand gestures, eye contact, facial expressions, and voice inflections. It's important to be aware of these influences because they communicate who we are and our attitude about teaching. Successful communication presumes a sincere respect for others, a quality that can't be faked, especially around children.

Sending out positive messages increases your effectiveness as a teacher. Positive messages take many forms and share important feelings of sincerity and caring.

"I am listening and I want to hear what you have to say."

"I am available to hear you when you need to be heard."

"I think what you have to say is important, and I care about you."

"I like who you are."

Negative messages, on the other hand, can decrease your effectiveness as a teacher and destroy your student's trust in you. Negative messages are sent, not only through our words, but through our actions.

"I am not listening even though I am pretending to."

"I am busy and I do not want to listen to you."

"What I have to say is more important than what you have to say."

"I really don't care."

Effective communication requires an awareness of the many messages we send and how we send them. As a teacher you will have the opportunity to touch your students' lives daily through your sincere and caring communication.

Communicating with Students

Whether consciously or not, you are always communicating with your students, both verbally and non-verbally. Keep your communication positive and caring. As a teacher you play an important role in the life of each of your students. Never make remarks to or around students that might hurt their feelings.

When you are first learning your students' names, think of a fun word, such as "jellybean" or "lollipop," as a substitute for a temporarily forgotten name. This is much more endearing than saying, "You in the blue shirt."

Greet each student as he or she arrives in the classroom. Use the child's name in your greeting and show enthusiasm. This helps children feel welcome and valued.

Call students by name as often as possible. Use their names in positive instances—not only when you admonish them.

Teach your class to respect the importance of a person's name. If a student has a nickname they like to be called, always try to use it. Do not allow students to call others by nicknames unless the individual agrees. Don't allow students to alter or shorten a classmate's name without his or her permission.

Children occasionally go through periods of wanting to change their names to something entirely different. Respect their desire, if it's not too distracting to class routine. The desire for a name change sometimes reflects a particular situation the child is experiencing and this is his or her way of processing.

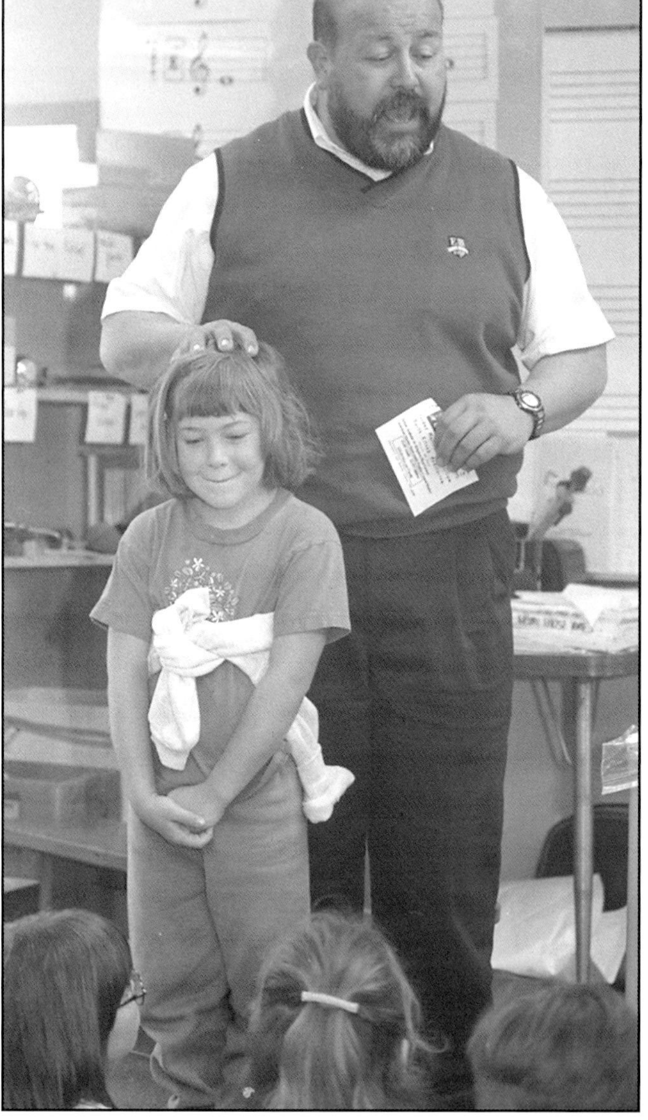

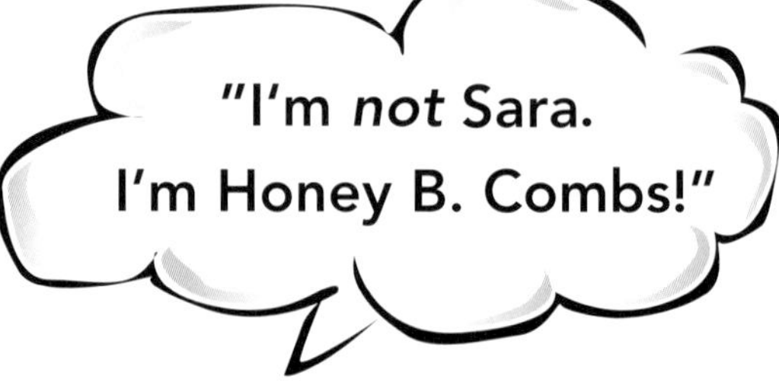

Remember, your students thrive on connecting with you. Take time to share "small talk," with them. Inquire about their dogs, cats, brothers, or sisters. Mention, to the class, if you see a student at the store, library, or soccer field.

Have a space on the blackboard or whiteboard where you write positive notes to the class, such as:

"I appreciate your hard work yesterday."

"I am looking forward to seeing your projects this afternoon."

"I feel like the luckiest teacher in the school."

Write messages on sticky notes to individual students and place them on their desks before they arrive at school. Appropriate notes might include a special thank you for a job well done; recognition of an effort made; a comment about a show-and-tell item; or, simply wishing them a happy day. Keep track of which students you have written to so that no one will be left out or overly favored.

Keep a pad of decorative paper in your desk to use on birthdays. Have birthday students come to the front of the room and dictate what they want you to write about their birthdays. It may include how old they'll be, what they plan to do to celebrate, how they're looking forward to turning a year older, what special treats they might eat, or what presents they hope to get. Students then take the paper home as a birthday remembrance. Be sensitive to children who may not celebrate birthdays and holidays.

Keep a supply of picture postcards to use as a special surprise. Two or three times a year, write a positive message to each student and place the card in his or her cubby-holes or mailboxes.

Keep a box in your classroom labeled "Teacher's Treasures." Keep all drawings, paintings, and paper gifts of love from your students. Storing them in this way helps children feel valued.

Encourage students to write to you. Have a mailbox or cubbyhole where students can place notes and letters to you.

Your communication is important, not only with your own students, but with all students in the school. Extend your communication beyond your own classroom by talking to students as you go down the hall or walk around the lunchroom. Take time to share a comment or ask a question. Don't let the fact that you do not know their names stop you from talking to them. Many students in your school will certainly know your name even if you don't know theirs. Establishing yourself as generally friendly and approachable cannot help but increase your effectiveness as a communicator and as a teacher.

Communicating with Students' Parents

The first few weeks of school is the time is to set the tone for future communication with parents. Let them know that you welcome their involvement in their children's education, and that you, as their child's teacher, want to stay in touch with them.

Early in the first week of school, send a letter home explaining your desire to welcome classroom visitors and volunteers. Tell them about newsletters and other communications they'll be receiving in the future. Provide them with the school phone number and let them know a convenient time to reach you. Give parents a list of supplies they'll need to provide, such as a box of tissues, towelettes, a water bottle, and postcards.

Maintain as much of an open-door policy in your classroom as possible. By welcoming parents, you encourage communication. Decide whether it's necessary for parents to inform you of an upcoming visit or if a "drop-in" visit is acceptable. This will be a personal preference and it may change from year to year. Once you've established a policy, apply it to all of your students' parents.

If you plan to use volunteers in your room, develop a system to organize work for them to do. A box with a lid can be used to store work. As parents enter the room, they'll get into the habit of checking for work or notes regarding jobs that need to be completed. Some parents prefer to work only with students, while others will be happy to do correcting or other work. Ask how they would like to spend their time and also how they would like the class to address them. Be sure to thank parents for all their help.

At the start of the school year, inform parents that they'll be getting daily reports on classroom activities. This can be done easily by having your students maintain a learning log or a daily calendar. Instruct students to write (or draw, depending on the grade level) three things they did that day. Encourage parents and students to talk about their activities. Have parents sign the daily calendar or log for students to return to school the next day. Continue this interaction throughout the week. On Fridays, students who have kept track of the calendar all week and have signatures can be rewarded. Rewards might be a sticker, a piece of candy, a coupon for free classroom time, or a spot on a special star-of-the-week chart. The rewards need to be appropriate to the children's age and your teaching style.

Ask parents to provide two stamped postcards addressed to themselves. Write an encouraging note home to parents, praising their child in some way. Choose a time when you can sincerely relate some positive occurrence or behavior. Parents and students love to get these special postcards in the mail.

Send all notices regarding activities or meetings home well in advance of the event. Nothing is more frustrating to a busy parent than to receive a last-minute notice. To be sure parents have received notices, include a section at the bottom for parents to sign, cut off, and return to school. For younger children, offer a sticker to those who return this signature.

Write a weekly newsletter to be sent home each Friday. Divide the paper into five days of the week. For each day report a memorable event. Include study topics, special events, and projects. Keep a simple format so you will be able to maintain the newsletter through the year.

Once a month take time to write a half-page note to parents, and make a copy for each student. Use a comfortable, easy-to-read style. These notes can be about a special classroom project, upcoming event, or an improved classroom behavior. This reminds parents that they are an important part of their child's classroom.

A great way to create lasting memories for parents and students is to make individual video recordings of each student. At the beginning of the year, have each child bring in a videotape labeled with his or her name. Whenever a child gives a report or a performance for the class, capture important moments on videotape. It's important to include the entire presentation or report. Explain to the class the need to listen quietly, as any comments or noises will be recorded. When taping is finished, the student may take the videotape home and show it to his or her family. Remind students to rewind tapes at home before watching, but not to rewind when they are finished watching. This way the tape is ready for the next taping. Tapes should be kept at school and only allowed to go home for one night of viewing. Your tapes can be passed on to next year's teacher for more recording, or sent home at the end of the school year as a keepsake.

Keep a stack of thank-you cards in your desk drawer so you can thank parents when they send in special items such as flowers, treats, or other things of interest to the class. Try to send the note home with the student the same day the time arrives.

At the beginning of the school year, and when you begin new units of study, it's important to keep parents informed of subjects to be covered. Explain your mode of communication, such as through newsletters and learning logs, to encourage two-way dialogue.

Communicating with Staff

Your colleagues, both teachers and staff members, can be a tremendous resource. Tap into their experience and insight by nurturing an open and friendly relationship. Make a point of knowing staff members' first names and job titles. A smile, a friendly hello, or sincere compliment about a special activity or display takes only a minute but can leave lingering warmth.

Keep a pad handy to jot down notes regarding special reminders or to just say hello. Using attractive or humorous paper can make the message stand out.

Use thank-you notes or postcards to express your appreciation. A hand-written note, rather than a printed message, goes a long way toward making someone feel valued.

Don't be afraid to ask questions. Teachers generally love to share information and will do so readily when asked. Asking questions is a great way to get to know others. Be willing to share your ideas as well. Offer staff members genuine "listening time" when requested.

Keep a list of staff members' birthdays (usually available from the school office). Make a point of wishing them a happy birthday or sending a card to celebrate the occasion.

Create an "Idea Folder" for staff members. Keep the folder in the library or staff room. The "Idea Folder" can be one file folder or several folders, each for a different topic such as teaching reading, art projects, math ideas, or discipline. The front of the folder(s) should be clearly labeled and have several pieces of blank paper inside. Encourage staff members to share their ideas by writing them on the paper. Have them write their names next to their ideas so they receive credit and can be contacted for more information.

CHAPTER FIVE

Organizing Paperwork

As a teacher you will never be short of paperwork. Not only will you have the paperwork generated by your students, but also paperwork that comes to you from your state educational offices, district offices, parents, clubs, conference networks, and companies you've never heard of.

Filing

You will have highly significant paperwork that requires your attention and focus. You will also have unimportant, redundant, irrelevant paperwork that does not merit your time or attention. Your goal is to know which is which, and to rid yourself of the rest. The best way to do this is to sort and file each paper as it comes to you. Try to avoid stockpiling papers to sort later. It is not only more difficult to sort large piles of paperwork, but it is also more difficult to store. Sorting items as they come to you is not only more efficient, it is habit forming. You will find that you can no longer tolerate large piles of paperwork looming around your classroom waiting to be sorted.

Sort your papers into three categories:

To Be Filed **To Be Read** **To Be Discarded**

Papers to be filed will be those that have information you want to keep on hand. This might be state or district information, school information, parent information or teaching tips. These papers can be filed in file folders and kept in your filing cabinet. Several file folders can be pre-marked and awaiting these papers. These folders could be labeled as follows:

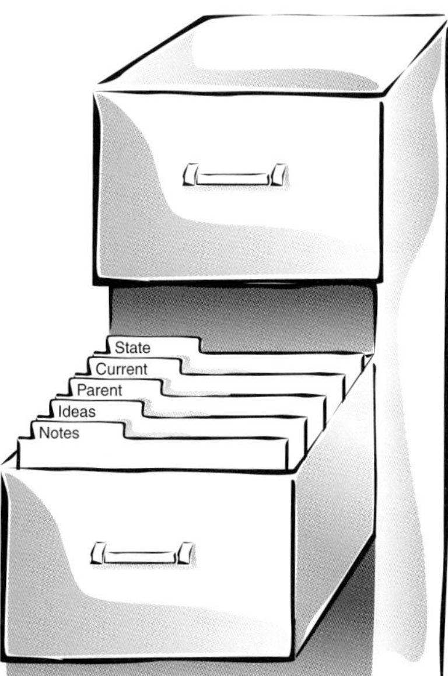

- State/District Information
- State/District Information CURRENT
- Parent/Student Information
- Parent/Student Information CURRENT
- (school name) Information
- (school name) Information CURRENT
- Programs/Courses/Conferences
- Ideas
- Notes and Cards
- Confidential

Folders bearing the label "Current" should contain information received during the current year. When the next school year begins, papers from the current folders should be reviewed. Any of the papers to be saved can be moved into the noncurrent folder. Any information no longer significant should be discarded.

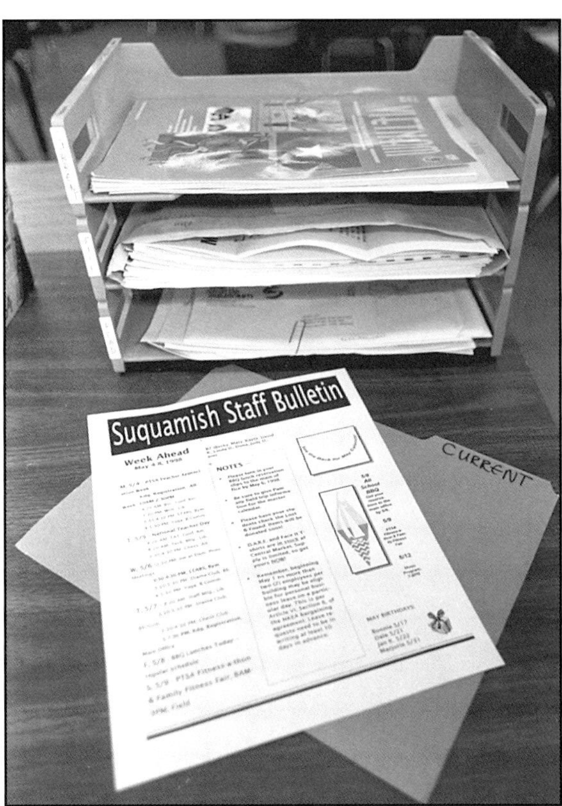

Folders labeled "Programs/Courses/Conferences" should be reviewed and sorted every few months. Information in this folder can become outdated quickly and needs to be thinned out.

The "Idea Folder" will continue to grow and grow. As it becomes full, sort it into subject areas. Keep a basket or folder at your desk labeled "Ideas to Use Right Away."

A folder labeled "Notes and Cards" should be added to each time you get an endearing note from a student, parent, or colleague. This is a great folder to pull out in those moments when you're overwhelmed and not feeling at your peak. Over the years, you'll enjoy looking back at the messages from those whose lives you've touched.

The "Confidential" folder should contain information that has been given to you in confidence or that you feel should be confidential. It may be information from parents or colleagues regarding students, or it may be information about topics you are researching and are not yet ready to share. Keeping the papers in this folder will help you to remember that the information is not to be shared freely.

If your school uses weekly bulletins, they should be kept for the week they are announcing. If they contain information about upcoming events, be sure to mark them on your calendar. Once the week is over, the schedule can be tossed out. If you need to refer to the schedule once the week is over, the office will have a copy of it.

If you have trouble throwing things away, you may prefer a more general filing system which allows you to keep most everything. You can have three folders with the labels:

Significant and Urgent

Significant But Not Urgent

Not Significant

Papers you can't decide how to deal with can be placed in a "Transition Box." This box can be stored in a cupboard where it is not highly visible. Once a paper is put in the "Transition Box" it can be retrieved if it gains importance. If the paper is not missed and gradually fades from your memory, you can then comfortably throw it away.

Absent Work

Keep a file folder labeled "Absent Work" in a resealable bag. Place the folder on the absent student's desk and place papers in it throughout the day. At the end of the day, the folder will be ready to slip into the resealable bag and sent home. The resealable bag can be decorated with permanent markers and stickers to make it look cheery. Replace both the bag and the file folder every few months depending on how much use it gets. It's a good idea to have at least three folders and bags ready to go in case of multiple absences.

Students who are absent miss valuable time in the classroom and important class work. In order to keep students up-to-date they need to have information about missed work.

To help students keep up with classroom work, send home materials in a resealable plastic bag, along with a note.

Part II
Behavior Management

CHAPTER SIX

Preventing Inappropriate Behavior

Prevention is often the best cure. This concept applies to behavior problems in the early childhood environment as well as to health and maintenance problems in the world at large. The five alternatives discussed in this chapter are particularly useful in nipping trouble in the bud.

Anticipate Trouble

Anticipating trouble is one of the most important alternatives; with it you can prevent trouble before it starts. Anticipating means knowing your students' personalities and developmental levels and being able to guess at their likely responses to various situations. Through anticipation, you can arrange materials and activities for students to use as soon as they arrive at school, thus motivating productive behavior. You can, in general, control the physical environment so as to minimize stress and promote trust and cooperation.

Anticipating also means being alert to the emotional environment. Sometimes the human elements of the environment are obvious, as in the case of students who elicit such comments as "Every time those two sit next to each other, they get into a fight." The anticipating teacher would make sure that those students did not sit next to each other.

Sometimes the emotional variables are more subtle and, therefore, less predictable. By carefully observing your students' interactions with one another, you will be able to tell by their body language and verbal communication when a situation is beginning to deteriorate. If they cannot solve the difficulty by themselves, your prompt intervention before trouble begins can prevent a serious confrontation.

The following are some examples of how anticipating trouble works.

Typical Response	**Anticipating Trouble**
You two boys stop that fighting right now. Every time you get next to each other you end up fighting. You heard me. Here! Tom, come and sit over here. I can't trust you two to be together. (The feelings generated are embarrassment, belligerence, tension, and lowered self-esteem.)	*Tom, you look rather comfortable over there, but for right now I'd like you to come and sit over here next to Susan.* (A tense situation is avoided politely and no negative feelings are generated.)
You get back here. You can't leave that stuff in such a big mess. Get that cleaned up right now. You should know that without my even telling you. (Again, the student feels embarrassed and tense, and the student's self-esteem is lowered.)	*We're going to get ready for lunch in a little while. As soon as you finish that row, you can start putting those things away. If you like, you can play with them again tomorrow.* (Caring and understanding are expressed, helpfulness is encouraged, and happy anticipation for the next day is set.)
Now see what you've done. You know you can't play ball next to those big windows. That's going to cost a lot of money to repair. (A window is broken, and students are made to feel fearful and guilty.)	*The window might break if the ball hits it. That would be dangerous. You may go over to that area to play. I'll be there in a few minutes. I'd like to watch the game.* (The teacher models appropriate caution, caring, and interest while averting trouble.)

It was three days before the winter recess and the holiday season. Students throughout the school were very keyed up, as were their parents and teachers. The staff discussed among themselves the importance of anticipating more irrational behavior on the part of the students than usual. They made plans for several steps that could be taken in anticipation of the heightened excitement and tensions.

Typical Response	**Anticipating Trouble**
Hurry up now. Everybody has to get to work. You'll never get these gifts done on time if you stand around talking. Here, who's working on this? Come on, come on. Don't waste so much time. Oh, my goodness. We have so much to do. I don't know how we'll ever get through the next three days. (The teacher is so keyed up that both her classroom planning and her own demeanor is adding to the already heightened tension of the students. The day will probably end up with several confrontations between the students and between the students and the teacher.)	*Here are several new puzzles and games that I've been saving for you. You can check them out for about half an hour. Then we'll go for a neighborhood walk, and later you can help me make a big smile collage for the whole school.* (Two weeks earlier, the teacher had sent home carefully mounted artwork that the students had done themselves. An accompanying note to the parents read, "Please help your child use this artwork in whatever gift-giving customs your family practices." The teacher has planned an interesting, low-key morning in anticipation of the students' heightened tensions. The walk helps use up surplus energy in a noncompetitive way.)

It had been indoor weather for five weeks. Today was the first day that the skies were clear and the students could go outdoors to play. However, five weeks of being indoors in very gloomy weather had put a lot of pressure on everyone, and both the students and the adults were very irritable.

Typical Response

Well, it's really a nice day for a change. It would be nice to go out and play, but you've behaved so badly, I think we'll just stay in until you learn the rules again. (Rather than helping these students regain their self-control, the teacher punishes them, possibly upsetting them to the point that their behavior will deteriorate even more.)

Anticipating Trouble

We're lucky that the weather has finally cleared up enough so we can go outdoors to play. First, let's go over some of our rules so we can really enjoy the nice day and have an especially good time playing together. (Anticipating that the students might be over-enthusiastic in their play after being indoors for so long, the teacher takes the time to review the school rules and limits with the students, thereby helping everyone enjoy their playtime more.)

Stevie, almost four years old, arrived at school in an unusually heightened emotional state. His family was preparing to move, and the moving truck was to come the next day. Everything at home was in a turmoil.

Typical Response

Teacher: *OK, Stevie, calm down now. I can see what kind of day we're going to have with you. Now you'll just have to straighten yourself out. You know, you're not the only one who's ever moved. People do it every day, and there's nothing wrong with it.* (Within five minutes Stevie has knocked one student out of her chair, and bitten another.)

Teacher: *I knew it. I want you to just sit at this table over here by yourself for the rest of the morning. That will straighten you out.*

Anticipating Trouble

Teacher: *Stevie, you're really excited about moving, aren't you? Here, let me rock you for a while and you can tell me about it.*

Stevie: (crying) *Where's Mamma?*

Teacher: *Your mamma went home to get everything ready for the truck.*

Stevie: *Are Mamma and Daddy going in the truck?*

Teacher: *No, Stevie. The truck man will come to your house tomorrow. You'll stay home tomorrow and see the truck come. Then Mamma and Daddy will go in your car with you. They can't go with the truck man.*

Stevie: *Can I go play?* (Anticipating his worries, this teacher puts Stevie at ease by helping him to express himself and by clarifying things for him before his emotions cause him to lose control of his behavior.)

Give Gentle Reminders

Gentle reminders are never sarcastic. Comments that are demeaning or embarrassing have no place in the development of wholesome interpersonal relationships. When they are properly conveyed, however, gentle reminders can fulfill for students the need to have someone on whom they can depend and to whom they can look for helping in maintaining their self-control.

Using Gerunds

Gerunds can be used as gentle reminders and are especially effective with preschool students. They also work well in pressure situations with older students.

If you say to a student, "We don't run in the halls," the student can respond with, "You don't run in the halls, but I do." If you say, "Don't run in the halls," the student can respond with, "OK. Later I won't run in the halls, even though I'm doing it now." But if you say, "Walking," the student will slow down immediately. The gerund has the same connotation as the command, "Stop running right now." Gerunds give you a method of seeking responses from students by use of the shortest, simplest, gentlest type of reminder. You can use them in virtually every situation.

The advantage of these and similar short phrases is that students seem to interpret them as really meaning "right now." The students respond to them easily; they appreciate the lack of lengthy tirades.

A helpful gerund reminder is "friendly playing." Whenever you see cooperative behavior beginning to deteriorate, approach the students and say, casually but definitely, "Friendly playing." It says to students, "I know you are capable of playing appropriately and

Typical Response	**Using Gerunds as Reminders**
Please sit down and wait.	*Waiting.*
Everyone is supposed to be helping to pick up the blocks.	*John, Susan, helping.*
Please sit still while I go get a storybook to read to you.	*Sitting quietly everyone.*
Jennie, please don't bother Armando. He doesn't like that.	*Leaving Armando alone, please.*
Watch out how you're carrying that. It's spilling.	*Carrying carefully, please.*
Keep your fingers out of those cupcakes. That's going to be for our party.	*Not touching.*
Don't just let it lie there on the floor. Pick it up.	*Picking it up.*
This is a quiet time. Everyone is supposed to be resting. Be quiet now, everyone.	*Resting.*
Please be quiet and listen.	*Listening.*
When I asked you to clean up this room, I meant for you to do it right now.	*Cleaning up.*

remembering the limits. I'll just give you a little reminder that will make the remembering easier for you." It is very effective with two-, three-, four-, and even five-year-olds. Time and again students will stop what they were doing, think for a moment, and then resume their activity with less belligerence or moodiness.

The effectiveness of gerunds is evident when you hear students use them with one another—especially when you see a little four-year-old looking at a group of peers and saying, "Friendly playing." Parents have reported that their children, when being nagged or lectured without having been given a chance to explain, will occasionally say, "Mother, listening" or "Waiting, please."

Some people have expressed concern that the use of gerunds as gentle reminders will result in students growing up using incorrect language. Hundreds of students go though this system to become excellent academic students. The use of gerunds as gentle reminders does not carry over into student's regular use of language; just as their teachers do, however, the students may call forth a phrase or two that suits their purposes when they need instant response.

The technique is especially useful with older students who have been consistently hard to handle. Children who are seven, eight, or nine years old and have frequent problems with their behavior may be surprised into cooperation by the use of gerund reminders as a new approach:

- To the student who is poised to run from the room before the bell has rung: "Waiting."
- To the student who walks up to another student with clenched fists, ready to start a fight: "Touching softly."
- To two students who have been quarreling and who are letting their emotions get out of control: "Discussing."
- To the student who is glancing at a neighbor's paper during a test: "Keeping your eyes on your own paper."
- To the student whose excitement is causing him to start off a string of crude remarks to another: "Using school words."

And to the teacher reading this book: "Trying it."

Reminding Older Students

Third graders and some older students respond well to reminders such as "Oh, oh! Remembering!" or "I'm watching you," or even just their names. As long as you are smiling, are not expressing anger, and are showing respect, they will usually reverse their actions and behave correctly. They can use gentle reminders with each other, too. In a discussion about improving their manners, a group of students agreed to give each other reminders by pointing the index finger up while saying "Ahhhhh." After a few humorous attempts at using this technique, they began simply reminding each other verbally, and kindly, not to be rude.

Nonverbal Reminders

Not all gentle reminders need to be spoken. Some effective nonverbal techniques for giving gentle reminders are:

- nodding your head
- catching a student's eye from across the room
- smiling as you gently shake your head
- touching gently on the shoulder

Avoid looking or sounding angry and threatening if you want to give students gentle reminders. Such conduct will remind students of the rules but may also encourage defiance, as the message is that you really don't trust or respect them. Your facial expression is very important. Think of your own response to people whose expressions are pleasant when they ask something of you as compared with people who look angry or hostile.

Distract to a Positive Model

This is yet another type of reminder. If it is not overused, distracting to a positive model can be extremely effective in helping students learn self-discipline. In early childhood settings, when a teacher becomes angry with one student it is not uncommon for another student to burst into tears. This can work for you in a positive way: When you notice something positive that one student is doing, another student, overhearing, may take it as a reminder to change his or her behavior so that it is similar to that of the student whose behavior was noticed.

In using this technique, you need to take care not to let the positive comment about one student sound like it is meant to humiliate, criticize, or deride another. The following examples show how this approach can be used much like a gentle reminder to help students opt for appropriate behavior.

Luis and Jeremy, both age four, are arguing over some puzzles.

Typical Response	Distracting to a Positive Model
Teacher: *If you boys can't share those puzzles, you just don't need to play with them. Here, give them to me.* (Luis and Jeremy learn that only the teacher has the power to punish them.)	**Teacher** (to Jedidah, age three): *Jedidah, I notice that you got one puzzle for yourself and shared one with Michael. That was really kind. Sharing is hard to do.* **Luis:** *Let's share.* **Jeremy:** *You can have that one.*

Tyler, almost four, is painting with tempera. He is pressing too hard with the brush and not getting the paint to flow smoothly.

Typical Response	Distracting to a Positive Model
Teacher: *No, Tyler, not that way. Can't you see what you're doing? You're not even painting. You're only ruining the brush. Stop. Here, let me do it for you. Now watch me.* (The teacher fails to tell Tyler the proper way to use the brush, but inspires him to walk away from the easel, totally disinterested.)	**Teacher:** *Oh, Tomiko! Look what happened when you held your brush gently! It looks like the paint is going where you want it when you move the brush slowly across your paper.* (Tyler glances over at Tomiko. He dips his brush in paint and starts over, trying not to press hard.) **Teacher:** *Wow, Tyler! Look how your paint is flowing so smoothly.*

Jack, age three, is having trouble quieting down for a nap.

Typical Response	Distracting to a Positive Model
Teacher: *I told you to put your head down and close your eyes. Don't you see that everyone else is trying to sleep? What's wrong with you today? I don't have time to pay attention just to you. I have all these other kids. Quiet down now.* (Pause) *Why are you crying? Stop that now, and go to sleep.*	**Teacher:** *Looks like lots of people are ready for a nap. I'll pat Debby, Tommy, Sammy, Justin, Cary, Susie, and Jack. Everyone is resting.*

Inject Humor

Humor is one of our greatest natural resources and should be used often with children. The finest teachers I know are people who have an active sense of humor. Too often adults, in appreciating the seriousness of their responsibilities, neglect this important aspect of communication. Children flourish when there is laughter, joy, and lighthearted repartee.

As children develop, they begin to appreciate jokes and riddles and continue to respond to silliness. They often get carried away with mimicry and clowning and let it overwhelm their original good intentions just to get some laughs going. Care needs to be used in balancing the use of humor with normal methods of communication.

In times of crisis or trouble, a note of humor can often alleviate a deteriorating situation and disrupt a pattern of growing tension. Laughter helps relieve tension and promotes a spirit of camaraderie.

In order to use humor and evoke joy, you need to project a cheerful attitude in the first place. Personal problems need to be put aside when you enter the classroom. You can display cheerfulness by your enthusiasm and optimism. You can let the students know, not only by what you say, but by your posture, demeanor, and your movements, that you are happy and enthusiastic about being at school and about being with them.

In using humor, avoid sarcasm. Never belittle anyone, but learn to laugh at yourself and have the students laugh with you. When you learn to laugh at yourself, you are declaring healthy "ownership" of imperfect behavior. Any time you can declare such ownership, it frees other people to admit their own imperfections and even to try to change their behavior. As in all interactions with students, the way we handle and use humor models for them ways they can handle and use it. Most important when injecting humor into a situation is remembering the importance of laughing with the students, never at them.

Choose Your Words

In using humor with students, take care not to use certain adjectives jokingly that may not sound so funny when students repeat them to their parents out of context and without your demeanor and expressions. For example, a teacher was heard to say, laughingly and in good-natured repartee with some four-year-olds coming in from the playground, "Come on, you sweaty little ragamuffins. It's time to clean up for lunch." The students laughed and cleaned up quickly and happily. But just think how it would sound if one of the students went home and said, "My teacher called me a sweaty little ragamuffin."

Consider Students' Individual Personalities

It is important to take the differences in students' personalities into consideration when using humor. Some children come from such solemn and serious homes that humor is very foreign to them. If used, it must be introduced gradually and with great gentleness. Such children may respond better to riddles than to outright jokes or kidding.

Some children may come from such economically and emotionally deprived homes that even though everyone around them is laughing, they don't realize that they can join in. These children are used to being out of the mainstream of society. They see without participating and look without wanting because they are accustomed to not getting. Their need for help in developing the ability to laugh and appreciate the funny side of things is great. They can't be forced into such attitudes, but they can be gently introduced to them, and given encouragement for even the slightest hint of a smile.

An especially good learning tool for students who are hesitant about humor is the smile mirror. It permits privacy while allowing for exploration. It should be put in a convenient place, one that is easily accessible to the students.

The following are steps for making and using a smile mirror:

Mount a small, unbreakable pocket mirror in the center of a 9" × 12" (22.5 cm × 30 cm) piece of cardboard.

Have the students help you cut out pictures of smiling faces from magazines.

Have the students help you paste the pictures onto the cardboard surrounding the mirror.

Have the students use the smile mirror as a plaything.

When appropriate, suggest that a student go get the smile mirror and see how he or she is doing.

Make two smile mirrors. A pair of smile mirrors allows students to enjoy this activity together.

Controlled, Caring Humor

Very young children have very simple levels of humor. They respond to silliness, mimicry, clowning, and other kinds of simple humor. Great care must be taken not to let such humor be mistaken for ridicule or deteriorate into chaos. On the contrary, controlled, caring humor can be a very productive means of distracting students from a negative situation.

Lighthearted Phrases

Not everyone is able to deliver humor with ease. If you aren't natural and comfortable with jokes and witty repartee, leave them to others—you can't fake things with children. You may, however, be more at ease injecting humor into everyday situations through the use of lighthearted phrases, as in the following examples.

Typical Response	Lighthearted Response
Everything seems to be going wrong.	*Well, look at me, will you? It's just not my day.*
No. It's easy to see that's not the way it goes.	*Oh, oh. We goofed that time, didn't we?*
Oh, I'm sorry. That's not what I really meant to say.	*Oops! I'm silly. I think I said what I didn't mean to say. Excuse me. What I really meant was . . .*
Now you just straighten up and listen to me. After all, I'm the one who's in charge and it's about time you understood that.	*Hey! Wait just a minute. I'm the teacher around here—I think!*
Oh, I forgot all about that. Well, it's too late now. I'll try to remember tomorrow.	*Sometimes I think I didn't really get up this morning, because I keep forgetting things. Do you want to touch me to see if I'm really here?*
Well, I don't know if those instructions were correct. Let me read them again.	*Oh, oh! I wrote it backward. This must be my backward day.*
Get up from there. Can't you see everyone is helping but you? Who do you think you are?	*Oh, oh, Are your muscles turning into noodles? I hope not. Come on. We really need your help.*
How dare you laugh at me. Can't you show any respect around here?	*What's so funny? Oh, I didn't realize I still had this clothespin on my sleeve. That's funny, isn't it?*

After all, there's enough seriousness in the world. Some gentle humor and lightheartedness can go a long way to helping us all through normally stress-filled days.

Lily, age three, slipped on some paste and went scooting across the floor on her bottom. When she came to a stop, she bumped the back of her head on the floor.

Typical Response

Teacher (laughing): *Oh, poor Lily. I'm sorry I'm laughing. You looked so funny!* (Lily, of course, cries loudly, her injury compounded by what she interprets as ridicule.)

Injecting Humor

Teacher: *Oh, my goodness. The floor must have moved and hit you in the head. Hey, floor! Stay still! Don't go around hitting children on the head.* (Lily, who has started to cry, is distracted long enough for the teacher to give appropriate aid and comfort without having to cope with a tantrum. In a minute, Lily is off playing with her friends.)

Lily (five minutes later, laughing): *The floor moved!* (She waits for the teacher to laugh with her before going back to playing.)

Mihn and Cheyenne were solving some math problems in a second grade classroom. John walked by their table and brushed against it, causing the table to jiggle and the children to react.

Mihn: *Why don't you watch where you're going, John!*
Cheyenne: *Yeah. Who do you think you are around here?*
John: *The boss, that's who.*

Typical Response

Teacher: *John, get back to your seat. And next time watch where you're going. I'll show you who's boss around here—and believe me, it's not you.*

John: *But I didn't mean to bump their old table. It was just an accident.*

Teacher: *Don't you talk back to me. Sit down and get to work.* (The three children get back to their work, but all are nervous and tense. John will probably repeat similar behavior because the teacher's excitement reinforces it.)

Injecting Humor

Teacher: *Come on, John, you know you're not the boss. I think you're an earthquake. Let's see you shake yourself all over like an earthquake.* (John shakes himself.)

Teacher: *Earthquake's over. They don't last long, do they?* (John stops shaking and goes back to his seat.)

Teacher (to girls): *Aren't you lucky he wasn't a bigger earthquake?*

John (returning): *I'm sorry. I didn't mean to bother you.*

Girls: *We know.* (A slight note of silliness keeps a minor incident in its proper, unimportant perspective. The teacher manages to get the three children back to their work totally relaxed.)

Jason and Ruben were painting side by side. Jason accidentally put his brush of yellow paint into Ruben's can of green paint. Ruben shouted, "Dummy! I'm going to mess your picture."

Typical Response

Teacher (grabbing Ruben's hand): *You'll do no such thing. How dare you. That's not a nice way to act. Now, you know he didn't mean to put his brush in your paint, so you'd better tell him you're sorry you called him a dummy. And don't you ever let me hear you talking like that around here. And Jason, I want you to watch what you're doing. Now you better tell Ruben you're sorry about the paint. Come on, boys, I want to hear you apologize to one another.*

Jason and Ruben (completely overwhelmed): *I'm sorry, I'm sorry.*

Injecting Humor

Teacher: *Look at that. Now we have two green paintbrushes. If you had three hands I could give you another brush and you could paint with three brushes at the same time.*

Ruben (laughing): *Yeah! And if I had a hundred hands I could paint with a hundred brushes!*

Jason (also laughing): *And I could use all the brushes.*

Teacher: *Here's a clean brush for the yellow paint. I noticed the way you have used all the parts of your paper for your pictures.* (By injecting humor into a simple problem, the teacher averts a major crisis. Ruben's anger, though legitimate, is not reinforced with a lecture about the word "dummy.")

Offer Choices

We are all involved in a continuous process of decision making as we pursue our daily lives. The more opportunity we have to make our own decisions, the greater our personal freedom. Children need help in learning to deal with the ongoing problem of making choices in order to learn to be discriminative. They need help in learning the possible consequences of the choices that are available. They need many opportunities to learn what is appropriate and what is not, what is safe and what is unsafe, what is right and what is wrong, what is wise and what is unwise. We need to help them learn, through training and practice, that they have the capability to make judgments and decisions on their own.

In giving such practice, it is wrong to punish students when they make errors in judgment. Rather, we need to look to our own methods of teaching and reevaluate the way we approach decision-making. The essential element in giving children choices is to be sure that all the choices we offer are acceptable. Choices must be offered with sincerity and honesty. Care must be taken that they are really choices and not threats. This is especially important when offering choices is used as a nonpunitive guidance technique.

The text box on the following page features examples of the difference between making threats and allowing students to make choices.

Typical Response	Offering Choices
You either pick up those blocks or sit in the time-out chair.	*You may pick up the blocks right now or you can come here, let me give you a big hug to show you how much I love you, and then pick up the blocks.*
You sure made a big mess. If you don't pick up those blocks right now, you won't be allowed to play with them again.	*You really used a lot of blocks today, didn't you? I know you'll feel better if you put them away neatly for the next person. Do you want to do it alone or do you want me to help you?*
If you don't put on your sweater, you can't go out today.	*You may put on your sweater. I can button it for you, Miss Mary can do it, or you may button it yourself. Those are really hard buttons to do.*
If you throw one more thing off your plate, you're going to have to sit in time out and not have any lunch.	*You may eat your lunch without throwing parts of it around or you may clear your place at the table and read a book while the others are finishing their lunches. Which will you choose?*
Stop that humming or else go sit out in the hall.	*You hum nicely, but it is hard to listen to your humming while we're trying to concentrate on our math. I need to have you stop now, but you can hum a song for us later today either at story time, after recess, or right after lunch. You don't have to decide now. Tell me later which you prefer.*
Stop grabbing those cars from Billy or I won't let you play at all.	*It makes Billy sad when you grab the cars from him. You may share them with him, go read a book, or come over here and play with this clay.* (Note: Clay manipulation has a calming influence.)

Just as important as giving choices is the importance of recognizing that making choices is a skill to be learned; very young children are often unable to make a decision. When faced with several options, they will become confused and indecisive. You may want to institute a program to help students learn how to handle decisions.

A Training Program for Decision-Making

A training program for decision-making should begin with giving students opportunities to make choices about things which affect only them. First on this agenda should be communication with the students' parents. Ask them whether they give their children opportunities to make choices at home.

Make a list of simple choices children could start with, such as:

- what shirt to wear to school
- which of three dresses to wear
- whether to drink milk with breakfast or after breakfast
- whether to have a bedtime story before getting into pajamas or after getting into them, and whether to read the story in bed or in a chair
- which story to read
- whether to color, play with dolls, or help dust
- whether to have an apple, a banana, or an orange
- whether to go to the store with Daddy or help Mommy in the garden
- whether to brush one's teeth before or after getting dressed

Parents are frequently amazed to realize that they have literally been telling their children every single thing to do, allowing no room for decision-making. Suggest that parents start by offering their children small choices, such as the ones in the list, to help children learn to handle decision-making.

Concurrently, you can begin a decision-making program in the classroom. Think ahead about situations in which you can offer children small, simple choices. Two choices are easiest for toddlers. For preschool-age and older children, try to give children three choices—one choice is no choice at all and two choices can be a dilemma. With only two possibilities, and both of them acceptable, it's really hard to make a decision or to weigh one against the other. With three choices, there is more room for thinking about consequences. The following examples may be helpful:

- You can sit in this chair, in this one over here, or on the floor.
- Here are three books. Which do you want to read?
- It's your turn to paint. You can start with the red or the blue paint or wait for this bright green I'm mixing.
- For snacks today, you may have either an orange, juice and crackers, or a piece of cheese and celery.
- Do you want to paint or do you want to play with the blocks? Or would you rather play on the climbing gym?
- Do you want to play with these alone, with Marisa, or with Joaquin and Marisa?

Gradually increase the complexity of the choices you offer, but never ridicule students when they have difficulty making a decision. Let them know that you don't want to make the decision for them. You can get this message across by giving them encouragement, saying, "Take your time" or "I can wait while you decide." Acknowledge that you realize that it's sometimes very hard to decide. Then support the student in carrying out the choice he or she has made.

Another step in teaching decision-making is to give the students opportunities to select the choices. For example:

- We're going to plant a garden. Here are pictures of several kinds of flowers we can plant. Which ones would you like us to choose?
- Tomorrow we are going to make lunch at school. What are the different kinds of sandwiches we could make? We'll have to decide on just one kind, or maybe we could have two.

Many times we make arbitrary statements that either give no choice or that make the children feel ashamed or inadequate. The box on the next page shows some examples.

Typical Response	Offering Choices
Here's a book to read while you're waiting.	*Here are some good books. You may choose one to read while you're waiting.*
Stop crying. Big boys don't cry.	*It's OK to be angry because your mother left. You may sit on my lap and cry or you may cry on the chair.*
Those lines are wide enough on that paper. You don't have to skip lines.	*Here's some paper to practice your spelling words. You may write a word on every line or you may skip a space in between.*
It's hard for some people to study when you're so noisy. If you don't quiet down I'll send you into the hall to do your work. (The teacher may think this is a choice, but it's more of a threat.)	*It makes it difficult for some people to concentrate when others are noisy. You may stay in here and study quietly, or you may study in the hall. Or, if you choose, you may bring your study book to me and I'll find a quiet place away from the others where you can read.*

One good way to help develop decision-making skills is to make art and play materials available and set them up so that the students have the freedom to use them in their own ways. Most teachers would say, "Of course I do that." Listed below, however, are comments picked up from teachers during a couple of extensive block-building sessions in which the teachers thought they were giving the students freedom of choice. They started out rightly enough, but then took that freedom away by negative comments and criticism.

Typical Response	Offering Choices
Why do you have to make so many small buildings? You can make one big building.	*It looks like you've chosen to build a whole city with lots of different buildings. That looks complicated.*
You always make the same kind of square building. You could use some other blocks to make towers and bridges.	*You have really learned to put together that kind of building quickly, haven't you? You could even choose to make a tower or a bridge if you'd like to.*
I don't think you should make a fort. That's for fighting. You should make a nice building or a house.	*You chose to make a fort. That's easy to recognize. That's an unusual kind of building to make.*
You're making the road too long. There really isn't room in here.	*Come and help me move some of these things out of the way. That will give you more room to make your road.*
If you don't get off those blocks you can't play with them anymore today.	*Brian, you actually made a chair out of the blocks! That's an interesting idea.*

Typical Response	Offering Choices
I think you need one large block in the corner or the whole thing will fall down.	*That's a very complicated building. You certainly know how to work hard. It might be a good idea to check this corner. What do you think will happen if that block falls?*
I told you it would fall. You should listen to older people. They can help you do things right. Hey! Don't you kick me! And don't you yell at me like that. If you had listened to me, it wouldn't have fallen down in the first place. I don't know what you're so mad about.	*I noticed that you decided to start right over when your building fell. I'm sure you can build that kind of building again. You've really learned how to put those blocks together. If you need help, just ask.*

Notice that in offering choices, the teacher uses words such as "choose" and "decide." Using these words helps children realize they are involved in the decision-making process.

Teachers frequently fall into the trap of thinking they are allowing children to make choices, when, in fact, they themselves are making all the decisions. The following is a typical example:

Teacher: *Boys and girls, Mr. Horace just prepared a garden plot for us near the little palm trees. We have to decide whether we want to plant flowers or food.*

Laura: *I think we should plant flowers so the room can always look beautiful.*

Corey: *Yes, and the outside will look beautiful, too.*

Teacher: *We can plant pumpkins.*

Josie: *But we can get pumpkins at the store. It's not so easy to get flowers at the store.*

Patricia: *We could plant lettuce and tomatoes and make our own lunch some day.*

Juan: *Yeah, and we can have carrots and have our own snacks.*

Teacher: *Don't you think a pumpkin patch would be nice?*

Laura: *I think planting lettuce, tomatoes, and carrots is a good idea.*

Jamal: *Then we'd know how to do it, and we could plant vegetables at home, too.*

Teacher: *Well, I think we should plant pumpkins so we can have our own pumpkins for Halloween.*

Mei Lin: *But it's not Halloween now.*

Teacher: *Yes, pumpkins will be nice. They're easy to grow.*

Patricia: *If we have our own pumpkins, then we can't go for a walk to Mr. Garner's pumpkin patch like we always do.*

Teacher: *Well I think we've had a very nice discussion, and so it's decided: We'll plant pumpkins.*

The children, who had been eager and interested at the beginning of the session suddenly became very quiet.

Teacher: *Now we'll have to have some committees. Who wants to be in charge of making sure that all the weeds are out?* (No response.) *OK, Bob, you can be in charge of that committee, and Tom and Mary can help you. Now, we need someone in charge of buying the pumpkin seeds. Who would like to volunteer?*

Laura: *I want to plant tomatoes.*

Teacher: *All right, Patricia, you be in charge of the buying committee. We'll walk over to the nursery next week and you can tell Mr. Lawson that we want a package of pumpkin seeds. Oh, my goodness, this meeting has taken so long it's already lunchtime. Thank you for helping us have such a good meeting. You all really know how to decide things.*

(Later, in the teacher's lounge)

Teacher: *Oh, we had such a good class meeting today. The children are really learning the democratic process. We had a discussion and they decided to plant a pumpkin patch. I'm so glad. I've wanted to have my own pumpkin patch for Halloween ever since I was a little girl.*

Unfortunately, that is exactly what it will be: the teacher's pumpkin patch. She will no doubt see to it that the children participate in its planting, upkeep, and even in its harvesting. But it will only serve as a lesson to them that they are incapable of making and carrying through plans of their own—they must be dependent on an adult.

How much more meaningful this project could have been if the meeting had been conducted in a truly democratic spirit, with all members honestly included in the decision-making process. It might have gone something like this:

Teacher: *Boys and girls, Mr. Horace just prepared a garden plot for us near the little palm trees. We have to decide what we want to plant. It could be flowers or food. Raise your hand if you want flowers. That's seven. Now raise your hand if you want food. That's seven, too. We'll have to discuss it to see which would be the best for all of us.*

Laura: *I think we should plant flowers so the room can always look beautiful.*

Corey: *Yes, and the outside will look beautiful, too.*

Teacher: *Let's hear from some of you who want to plant food.*

Patricia: *We could plant lettuce and tomatoes and make our lunch some day.*

Juan: *We can have carrots, too, and have our own snacks.*

Laura: *I changed my mind. I think planting lettuce, tomatoes, and carrots is a good idea.*

Teacher: *What do you think about maybe planting pumpkins?*

Patricia: *But we always have so much fun walking to Mr. Garner's pumpkin patch to get pumpkins for Halloween.*

Mei Lin: *He's so nice. I like going there. He likes kids.*

Teacher: *Thank you for reminding me. I had forgotten all about Mr. Garner. We certainly don't need two pumpkin patches for Halloween, do we?*

Jamal: *Let's take another vote.*

Teacher: *OK, how many still want flowers? Let's see . . . only three. Well, I guess vegetables are what we'll plant. In fact, we can plant a few flowers around the edge of the garden. How's that?*

Juan: *Can I be in charge of pulling out all the weeds and getting the ground ready? My Dad and I do that at home.*

Teacher: *I'm glad you volunteered for that job. Who wants to be on his committee?*

By listening and giving the children an honest choice without imposing her own will, this teacher has helped these children increase their decision-making skills and grow in their understanding of the democratic process. For these children, small choices will be easier. Giving choices as a means of intervention will also be easier and more easily accepted by them.

Children who have been given choices in early childhood will be more tolerant of one another because they recognize that there are alternative ways of doing things. As they progress in their educational life, they will be skilled in making decisions about what classes to take in higher grades, what kinds of friends to choose, how to dress, and all of the other options that are available to youth today. They won't find it necessary to listen to everyone who claims to be a leader. Because of their experience, they will be better able to discriminate between good leadership and bad—they will know better when to follow, when to choose another option, and when to take the lead.

When There Is No Choice

Just as important as helping children make choices is helping them to recognize that there are times when you can't give them a choice. You need to be clear and explicit in saying "This is what you're going to do today. Because of the weather, there is no choice. We can only play indoors," or "Some other time you can have a choice. Because it's almost time to go home, I've picked out this short story to read for you." Notice that in telling children there can be no choice, the reason for not giving a choice is also given.

CHAPTER SEVEN

Communicating With Children

As described in Chapter 4, what we say and how we say it are critical in dealing with children. The ways we communicate with children, both verbally and nonverbally, are, generally speaking, under our control and thus can be used as tools for guidance. This chapter focuses on what we say to children, how we say it, and how they are likely to respond.

Notice Positive Behavior

Every human being wants to feel respected, admired, cared for, and appreciated. When others reassure us that we are appreciated, worthwhile, liked, capable, and accomplished, our self-esteem increases. When someone we trust points out the things we have done well, our self-esteem increases. When we make mistakes, however, we may feel guilty about not having lived up to our own or others' expectations. Dwelling on our mistakes can make us feel like failures; the resulting lowered self-image can foster such behaviors as tension, clumsiness, confusion, aggression, and withdrawal. Helping students recognize their accomplishments, no matter how small, teaches them to appreciate their worthiness and potential and helps them develop serenity in their attitudes toward school. It also encourages ambition in their attitudes toward learning and determination in their desire to achieve a positive self-image.

Students who are constantly criticized may feel that they may as well give up trying, that they have no hope of achieving success. Such students may test—that is, try to prove—their unworthiness by behaving even more badly than they had in the first place; they try to live up to their poor self-images. Inappropriate behavior often increases when such students receive empty praise—praise that tells them how wonderful they are when they know that they have done something that is unacceptable.

The following considerations should be taken into account in developing the habit of noticing students' positive behavior as an alternative to either criticizing or offering empty praise:

When commenting on a student's accomplishments, be sincere, not condescending. Don't say "That's a beautiful painting," when you really think it's ugly. You could say, "I notice you covered the whole paper with paint. That must have taken a lot of work." This is a positive, honest comment that does not evaluate the painting.

Use as few words as possible. If you say, "Oh, how wonderful! Isn't that great! You really did that very nicely. That was good," the gushiness overwhelms the student. A simple statement about a specific aspect of a child's work is easier for the child to accept: "Look at that block building you made. You must be very proud of your work."

Avoid the trap of using praise instead of noticing positive behavior. Concentrate on behavior that shows new steps in growth, development, or learning. Once you've mentioned a particular achievement to a student, you don't have to dwell on it every time the student repeats the act. For example, if you tell Habeeb every day, "You cleaned up the block area today. I'm so proud of you. You're my best cleaner-upper!" Habeeb may eventually reply, "You already told me." Tired of being told how proud you are of him, Habeeb is just about ready to stop cleaning up the block area. A more effective statement may be, "Habeeb, I noticed you've finished cleaning up the block area. You're ready to go outside to play." The clean block area is duly noted, but not praised. Habeeb has already learned that he knows how to effectively clean up the block area and it makes him feel proud of himself to be able to do it without reminders.

Noticing positive behavior should not be confused with flattery. Flattery is used to wheedle, trick, or coax something out of someone. For example, a teacher might say, "I just love those drawings you made. You're such a good artist. You'll probably be a famous artist when you grow up. Oh, how lovely! Those are so pretty. I just love them," to wheedle the student into offering a drawing. Honest, objective comments on aspects of the student's work is more likely to inspire the student to keep doing her best: "You've made a lot of flower pictures today. I see red ones and green ones and purple ones, too. Let me know if you need more paint."

Comment on the effort that students make, not on innate intelligence. If you say "How did you do that so quickly? You're smart. I don't know how you do it," you don't give the student an impetus for future action. But if you say, "I notice that you figured out what you wanted to do and then went right ahead and finished it. That was hard," you give the student encouragement to try other hard tasks.

Comment on what students do, not what they are. "You followed directions so quickly" is preferable to "You're my best boy today."

Comment on what students may accomplish rather than on what they may acquire. To say, "Oh, what a beautiful doll. You're certainly a lucky little girl," emphasizes the doll. Compare it with this statement, which focuses on the child's behavior: "I can see by the way you're carrying your doll that you're going to be able to take good care of babies some day."

Although many tasks require conformity, students should be acknowledged when they display originality and creative thinking. If you say, "You didn't make the tree the way I showed you. I'm very disappointed in you," the students will not enjoy drawing. But if you say, "Wow! Look at the many different kinds of trees you all made," the students will grow with their creativity.

Comments on positive behavior should always be directed to the person involved, rather than to others within hearing distance. To announce to a co-worker, "Aren't they all doing nicely?" puts the students in the position of eavesdropping and withholds from them the pleasure of being addressed individually and honestly. If you say to the students, "You are all turning the pages of the books so carefully," their self-esteem gets a boost and they double their efforts.

Noticing positive behavior should be done discreetly. Noticing a student's accomplishments should not be an embarrassment to the student you've noticed, and it should not imply the inadequacy of others. If you say, "Everyone look. Isn't this a beautiful painting that Justin just made? Isn't he a good artist?" Justin will feel embarrassed and the other students will feel less adequate. If you say, "Justin, you've balanced the light and dark colors so that they make an interesting design," you give Justin critical insight as well as acknowledging his efforts without embarrassing him, and you may inspire others who overhear to experiment with light and dark colors.

Touching Students When You Notice Positive Behavior

When you acknowledge student's positive behavior, especially those with low self-esteem, touch them gently. A gentle pat on the shoulder or arm when you make positive comments on their accomplishments will invoke warm feelings when you touch the student in the same way in the future. The touch alone will remind them of their capabilities.

Noticing Positive Behavior in the Hard-to-Reach Child

Stefan, age five, seldom was acknowledged for positive behavior. He was a child with behavior difficulties who frequently bothered others, ignored directions and limits and behaved in a general antagonistic and antisocial way. His teacher decided that she would spend one entire day trying to help Stefan find a way to behave positively so that she could acknowledge his efforts. Her hope was that he would like the positive interaction and continue to act more cooperatively.

Stefan liked books on dinosaurs. One morning, as soon as Stefan entered the classroom, his teacher gave him a new book about prehistoric animals. She also gave him a handful of paper strips.

Teacher: *Stefan, please do me a favor. This book has many pictures of prehistoric animals, but I need to know which ones are dinosaurs. Would you put one of these yellow paper strips on each page that has a picture of a dinosaur on it? I really appreciate your help.*

Intrigued with the illustrations, Stefan attacked the job with gusto. He became absorbed in the assignment and did the job well. Stefan's posture indicated that he sensed he was doing it right. Before he finished, the teacher approached him and the following conversation ensued:

Teacher: (patting Stefan on the shoulder) *You certainly are working hard. I didn't realize there were so many pictures of dinosaurs in that book.*

Stefan: *I found all the pictures. I know how to read "dinosaur." I could use another color paper to put on the pages that tell about them.*

Teacher: (again touching Stefan on the shoulder) *That would help! Thanks for suggesting it. Here are some blue strips.*

Stefan: (after working diligently for half an hour) *Here's the book. I did a good job.*

Teacher: *Thank you. You followed the directions just right. You may have that book any time you like. Maybe you'd like to make some dinosaur pictures for our bulletin board. You can be in charge of that.*

Stefan: *Me?* (He'd never been in charge of anything.)

Teacher: *Yes. That would brighten up our room a lot.*

Stefan: *I'm sure glad I came to school today.*

For approximately one hour, Stefan was cooperative and pleasant. As he began to slip into his old patterns of behavior, the teacher walked quickly to him, gave him a gentle pat on the shoulder and said, "Remembering."

The teacher followed up the day's ego-boosting experience with similar experiences for the next few days. Each day, the carry-over into positive behavior lasted longer and longer. When Stefan did forget, it required merely a touch on the shoulder, a gentle reminder ("Remembering"), and, finally, just a glance from across the room for the teacher to remind him. As his negative behavior occurred less frequently, the teacher began to ignore that behavior completely, giving him more and more acknowledgement for cooperative behavior. At the end of the second week, the teacher knew she had made progress in helping Stefan's self-esteem when he volunteered to clean up some spilled water.

When You're Not Used to Acknowledging Positive Behavior

Some teachers say that they are not used to noticing positive behavior because they have so many poorly behaved students. In such cases, it's good to start out by looking for very simple accomplishments and commenting on them.

When a student hangs up his coat instead of dropping it on the floor, say "You took good care of your coat by hanging it up."

When a student completes a puzzle and returns it to the shelf, say, "You put the puzzle back on the shelf. That really helps our room stay neat."

When two students work cooperatively on a block structure say, "I notice the way you two are working together. What a tall building you're making!"

Acknowledging Children's Feelings

Acknowledgement of children's feelings gives them positive feedback on the directions in which they are making positive growth. This helps children recognize their power to develop positive patterns of action. Establishing a climate in which positive feelings are noticed and commented on can go a long way toward minimizing the frequency of antisocial behavior.

The examples on the next page show how children can have their feelings acknowledged. Read the first two examples. Then think about how you would respond to remaining ones.

Child's Action	Teacher's Comments
Ysidro gives you a big smile.	*Ysidro, you have a happy smile today.*
Tamara enters the room with unusually erect, confident posture.	*Tamara, you look like you're feeling good today.*
Kayla brings Li to you for treatment of a scraped knee.	____________________
Shari opens her thermos without help for the first time.	____________________
Jesse gives Murphy half his sandwich when Murphy's falls in the dirt.	____________________
Johari picks up blocks and puts them away even though the other children who had been playing with the blocks ran off to play outdoors.	____________________

Noticing effort and accomplishment

When you and the students are comfortable with acknowledgement of feelings, you can begin to supplement comments with simple statements of fact about particular efforts or accomplishments. The following are examples of such statements:

Typical Response	Noticing Positive Behavior
You missed eight words. I want you to write each of them ten times to help you learn their correct spelling.	*You learned four new words today. You can study four that you missed and try those again tomorrow.*
Well, it's about time you remembered to bring your homework.	*I see you remembered your homework today. Thank you.*
Juan spilled those. You don't have to pick them up.	*You're helping Juan pick up his beads.*
When are you ever going to learn to button your own sweater?	*You put your own sweater on. I'll button the top buttons and you can try the bottom ones.*
You better watch your language. You know our rules about hurting words.	*I notice you stopped yourself when you started to say an unkind word. Thank you.*

Nonverbal and Indirect Ways to Notice Positive Behavior

Verbal comments are not the only way to acknowledge a student's positive behavior. There are many nonverbal and indirect methods that can be used to build and reinforce children's good feelings about themselves. Here are nonverbal methods:

- Smile
- Nod encouragingly
- Provide a gentle squeeze, hug, pat on the shoulder or arm

To acknowledge a student's positive behavior indirectly:

- Give the student a leadership task
- Give the student a difficult task, knowing that he or she will be able to accomplish it

Offer Encouragement

Encouragement is closely related to noticing and acknowledging a child's positive behavior. Encouraging children is another way of helping them learn to respect themselves. It is a way of saying that their efforts are valuable and they can accomplish many things at their own levels, not in comparison to others. Encouragement bestows motivation. It gives us renewed energy, faith in ourselves, courage to attempt or continue difficult tasks, and independence to reach out for new levels of achievements.

Because our world is filled with uncertainty, even under the most ideal circumstances, children are prone to self-doubt. Our goals should be to promote children's independence of action, self-confidence, and awareness of their own capabilities. We need to think in terms of raising courageous persons who can face the vigorous challenges of a rapidly changing society. Through encouragement we can help children learn to surmount their problems. We can acknowledge the difficulty of a situation and help them learn that, through perseverance, industriousness, and practice, they can overcome obstacles.

In giving encouragement, we can help students set realistic goals for themselves based on their individual capacities and personalities. We can help them learn that to do one's best is a valid goal as long as it is sincere. Such learning will keep students from giving up when things seem to be getting more difficult. They will gradually build their skills in accordance with their growing capabilities, acquiring self-respect and strength of character at the same time.

Encouragement should be based on what you observe to be student's efforts or struggles; it should not be judgmental nor tied to past failures. Look at what is going on at the moment and address your comments to that.

Disparaging remarks, sarcasm, and denial make students feel worthless. The students may develop hostile and belligerent attitudes and feel so discouraged that they give up trying to achieve goals. The following examples show how encouragement can be used as a method of discipline and guidance:

Encouragement must be sincere. Don't pretend something is hard when it's not—that says to students that you don't think highly enough of them to be honest, that you think they are incapable and unworthy. Use encouragement to allow students the pleasure of knowing that some things are indeed easy for them to do and the security of knowing that

Typical Response	**Offering Encouragement**
Hurry up. Finish that. It's easy. (This is not an honest appraisal of the student's effort.)	*That's very hard. Take your time. Let me know if you need help.* (This acknowledges the difficulty of the task as well as the teacher's belief that the student can succeed.)
Come on. You can do it. Tanner just did. (This comment implies that Tanner is "better.")	*That takes a lot of practice. Tanner had to try many times before he could do it.* (This gives the student hope that, through practice, she can learn and succeed.)
Everyone else can do it. I don't understand why it's so difficult for you. (This belittling remark implies there is something wrong with the student.)	*Many other students are having a difficult time with those problems, too. Just do as many as you can. I know they are very hard, and I appreciate your wanting to try.* (This encourages the student to try difficult things.)

Typical Response	Offering Encouragement
Why don't you watch what you're doing when you throw the ball? (This implies the student is stupid.)	*Learning to throw balls where you want them to go takes a lot of practice.* (This encourages the student to practice.)
That's silly. You don't have to be afraid of a little thing like that! Come on now. I want you to carry that jar for me. (This denies the student's fear and does not help overcome it.)	*It's all right to be afraid. Some spiders bite and it's important to be careful. Handle the jar very, very carefully. That's right.* (This puts the most positive light possible on the student's handling of fear.)
There's no reason for you not to stand up and tell the entire class. If you don't do it, you'll have to miss recess. (This denies the student's anxiety and makes a threat; it does not help overcome a legitimate problem.)	*Many people find it difficult to talk to groups. Maybe you and Sharnelle can practice with some small groups, maybe just five or six of us; that will help you get used to it.* (This helps relax a student who is uneasy about speaking in front of a group.)
Well, you got that far; you would be able to finish if you weren't so lazy. (This belittles the student's efforts and character.)	*That was hard, wasn't it, to get as far as you did. Just keep plugging away, little by little, and you'll have it all done.* (This encourages perseverance.)
I told you you wouldn't be able to do it. Now see the mess you've made? (This dwells on the student's error and causes humiliation, compounding the problem.)	*That was really too many to carry, but I know you were trying to help. Just pick them up and take them in two trips. There's plenty of time.* (This acknowledges failure but also good intentions; it offers a solution to the problem.)
Here, give me that. I'll put it on for you. (This denies the student independence.)	*That sweater is hard to put on over your long sleeves, isn't it? Here, I'll show you how to hold the underneath sleeve so you can do it yourself.* (Your willingness to help prevents frustration.)
If you don't tell the truth here in front of everyone, you'll just sit here until you do. (Threats and punishment overwhelm the student and the original problem.)	*When we make a mistake, it's embarrassing to tell someone about it. It's ok to talk to me. I've made lots of mistakes myself. The door is closed and no one else can hear us. Can you tell me about what happened to Marsha's pen?* (Reassurances encourage a student to talk about a problem.)
Now, it's been a whole week since your dog died. Enough of that nonsense. I'm tired of it. (Lack of sympathy shames the student.)	*I know you're still sad about your dog. You loved him so much. You really need to do your work right now, and maybe later we can talk about the dog again and about how much you miss him.* (Your sympathy consoles the student, at least temporarily.)
I don't care how you feel. We're all going and you'll just have to come along. (This denies the importance of the student's own feelings.)	*I know you don't like to go on the bus. Sometimes it can be scary. It's all right to be upset about it, but I need you to go with the rest of us. You can sit next to me. I know you can be very brave.* (This acknowledges the student's feelings, but encourages his or her cooperation.)

when something is difficult, you will acknowledge the difficulty and provide support or assistance.

Encouragement need not always be verbalized. A nod, a smile, a touch of the hand, standing nearby— all of these can give students courage to continue a difficult task. Your tone of voice, too, can convey your true feelings, so when giving encouragement, be sure that your voice carries the meaning you are trying to get across.

Clarify Messages

Clarifying messages is an important alternative method of discipline. Not only does it mean good communication, but it can prevent misunderstandings. Clarification means that when you request things of students, you do so in clear, precise terms that leave no room for misunderstanding. Compare the following examples:

Unclear Message

This room is a big mess. (Five minutes later.) *I said, this room is a big mess. Didn't you hear me? You can just spend your outdoor play time cleaning up the room.* (The students were supposed to infer that the teacher expected them to clean up the room. Small children's minds don't work that way. When they didn't respond, the teacher became angry, inflicted punishment, and finally—after all that—told the students to clean up the room.)

Clear Message

I expect you to pick up the toys and put them where they belong right now. (Five minutes later.) *You've done a good job of cleaning the room. Thank you.* (Not only did the students know immediately what was expected of them and when it was expected, but, because of their immediate response, they received positive feedback.)

Obtain the Students' Attention

Before you make any requests, be sure you have the student's attention. You can do this by singing a song, gently striking a triangle, or by going quietly from one learning center to another, talking with students in small groups, rather than addressing the whole group at once. If you fail to get their attention, you'll find yourself repeating requests over and over again. When you become angry enough, your voice will rise to a pitch that will finally get their attention. The students will listen, but you may be so emotional that your effectiveness will be lessened.

Use Language the Students Can Understand

Be sure, in making requests, that the students can understand what you are asking. Consider their individual abilities and development. Don't expect three-year-olds to respond with the understanding of five-year-olds. Don't expect fours and fives to respond with the logic of sixes and sevens. Keep your words as simple as possible. State exactly what you want the students to do. Be explicit. If you want them to move their chairs, say so. If you want them to get their sweaters and jackets on, say so. If you want them to listen carefully to what you are saying, tell them so.

Students must also understand exactly when you expect your request to be acted on. Be specific—use phrases like "right now," "in five minutes" (provided they know what five minutes is), "before lunch," "before you go outdoors," "when the bell rings," and similar explicit statements.

Consider Developmental Capability

Many times poor response to teachers' requests relates to children's development. Children are often asked to do things that they have not yet learned. Although many children can learn to tie their shoes before five years of age, it is generally a five-and-a-half-year-old's accomplishment. It takes until approximately three years of age for children to develop good control of their shoulder muscles and the muscles leading from the shoulder to the wrist; it takes another two to two-and-a-half years (or to about age five and a half) for them to develop good finger control.

Frequently asking students to do things that they are not physically ready to do does not give them appropriate challenges. Instead, it can be discouraging, create poor self-images, and lead to patterns of poor response even when the tasks become easier to accomplish. The teacher must find a balance between what students are already able to accomplish and the next challenging—but attainable—step in growth.

Consider Intellectual Capacity

Some children may be physically ready for certain tasks, but they may not be ready intellectually. Some children are slower than others in processing information. A child may have a mild learning difference, or even have some strong emotional problem that interferes with the ability to concentrate on what is being said. Teachers who take these kinds of factors into consideration will not always expect an entire class to respond to the same type of communication. Such teachers will make allowances for students who need extra help. They will gear their requests to levels which all the students in the classroom can understand or they will give requests individually, as needed, to ensure the directions are understood.

Use Consistent Wording

Be consistent in the type of wording you use for certain routine or everyday requests. Consistent wording can save a lot of misunderstanding between teachers and the students in their classes. If you develop certain stock phrases, the students will be able to respond to them with relative ease because they will have heard those particular requests over and over again. Using stock phrases for routine tasks can free you to carefully consider exactly how meaningfully you can word requests for non-routine tasks. Also, consistency gives security to children who live in a world of rapid changes.

Give Nonverbal Reinforcement

Use body language to reinforce your verbal messages. For example, lean forward slightly to show your interest. This is especially important when dealing with children who are not accustomed to responding to adult requests. To avoid being defied or ignored by the students, it is important that you look directly at their faces.

Whenever possible, avoid talking to large groups of students. With groups of ten or fewer, your chances are much greater of getting each child's attention. Use individual student's names frequently, so that they understand that you are addressing them, too.

When talking to a student who has difficulty responding to requests, touch the student gently on his or her shoulder or arm. This increases sensory awareness. As the brain receives the touching message, other areas of the brain become more alert, and you are more apt to get an immediate response.

Be Patient and Understanding

Your patience will help students learn to respond to your requests without arguing or balking. Show the students that you understand that it takes a long time to grow.

Sometimes it may be important to verbally acknowledge students' feelings at the same time you are letting them know your expectations. You might even find it helpful in some situations to express your own feelings about a particular request you are making. (See "Offer Encouragement," earlier in this chapter.)

Clarify Messages

Clarification is a two-way street. While you are improving your own skills in telling students exactly what you want and when, you can improve their skills in doing so, too. Some of their skills will develop as they imitate your modeling, but you can further help them by having them practice giving you messages that state exactly what they want to tell you. Also have them practice including time elements in their requests when appropriate. Saying when to do something makes the message even clearer.

You can make up instructive games to play with young students; for example, give the students a garbled message and have them try to clarify it. Older students can play the same kind of game, with the students taking turns making up the garbled messages. For example, "eggs today bought store at I the" means "I bought eggs at the store today," and "ready the o'clock list be ten will at" means "the list will be ready at ten o'clock."

The following are examples of messages that can easily be misunderstood. Read the first two examples. Then think about clear, precise messages for the remaining examples.

Unclear Messages	What The Teacher Wants	Clear Message
Everyone get ready if you want to go outdoors. ("Get ready" is not a specific request.)	*I want them to put on their coats and sweaters.*	*Please put your coats and sweaters on so we can go outdoors before it starts to rain.*
Those books don't belong on the floor. (This is a statement, not a request.)	*I want her to pick up the books and put them on the shelf immediately.*	*Please put all of the books back on the shelf right now.*
How dare you. That's not very nice.	*I want her to stop spitting at Tommy right now.*	____________
I'll just wait until everyone is quiet.	*I want everyone to be quiet now.*	____________
People aren't going to like you if you keep acting like that.	*I want her to stop poking Felicia while I'm reading the story.*	____________
You'll have to miss recess if you can't straighten up.	*I want him to stop throwing spitballs around the room now.*	____________
Why don't you grow up?	*I want them to stop climbing on the chairs this minute.*	____________
Well! I'm certainly ashamed of you!	*I don't want him to use vulgar words in the classroom.*	____________
Can't you see you're bothering me?	*I want him to wait until I'm finished talking to Gloria before he asks his question.*	____________

CHAPTER EIGHT

Problem-Solving Strategies

When you are faced with problems in the classroom, how do you begin to solve them? So many factors are involved in running a classroom, and so many things can go wrong, that even little problems can sometimes appear impossible and overwhelming. This chapter provides a process by which these challenges can become manageable.

If you're feeling overwhelmed by the challenges of teaching, the more concrete and specific you make them, the easier they are to approach and solve. Just as an enormous house cleaning job becomes much less threatening when you break it down into smaller, separate tasks in individual rooms, so the job of teaching becomes more manageable when you divide it into separate tasks.

To begin, you may want to separate what you want to work on into "interactive" and "noninteractive" categories. This chapter examines problems in teacher-student interactions, usually called "student behavior problems." The process described is designed to help you isolate—and approach—one specific problem with one specific student. Eventually, you may wish to apply the process to solving problems with other students or to problems that are not specifically related to students.

The process involves isolating a problem, defining and documenting it, and then implementing and evaluating various solutions. Working through the process has several advantages, including the fact that you are likely to remedy a problematic situation. Along the way, you may feel better about the fact that you are at least trying to solve the problem. If you then discover that the problem is beyond what you are capable of dealing with in the classroom, you have solid documentation to support a decision to enlist outside help. Consider the following steps for problem solving.

Step 1

Try to define exactly what the problem is. For example, "Michael always seems to be out of his seat," is far more specific, and therefore easier to work with, than "Michael is driving me crazy." Although Michael may have a number of other problems, start with the one that is most disruptive or annoying.

Try to focus on what you can observe in the classroom. Dealing with disruptive behavior that occurs in your classroom is important even when it may be caused by things outside of your classroom, such as the birth of a new sibling or a divorce. Understanding outside influences will be helpful, yet they do not excuse unacceptable behavior, nor will they change the fact that the behavior is disturbing your classroom.

Step 2

Now that you have identified a specific problem, begin collecting data to document its existence and describe its depth, dimensions, frequency, and impact on other students. Do your data collecting before you make any changes in your behavior; you simply want to determine how bad the problem is. For example, Ms. Montoya, a first grade teacher, determined, simply by making marks on a piece of scratch paper, that a student she was observing was at her side with a question or interruption more than forty times between the morning bell and the first recess.

By collecting data, you may discover that what had seemed to be a big problem either has improved or wasn't as big as you had originally thought. Is Gloria *always* difficult, or just when she tries to work with art supplies? Is Ron always noisy, or just after physical education? How long has it been since Danita was in a fight? Although the student will probably be the primary source of data, you may wish to examine other sources, such as parents, support staff, former teachers, or cumulative folders.

Use various strategies to collect data about the student's performance, behavior, and attitudes. Select strategies that will give you the most useful information about the problem you have identified. Depending on the problem you are studying, you may compile anecdotal records; collect work samples and results of diagnostic or placement assessments; or administer student interviews and inventories, time-on-task studies, or sociometric assessments.

You may want to use the same strategy at different times, or for several days, to determine consistency. Ms. Montoya, for example, might observe her student's behavior during the next few mornings, in other classes, or between lunch and dismissal. As you collect data about a particular student, file the materials in a separate folder for that individual.

Keep in mind that the purpose of data collection is not to produce a weapon against the student. The only reason you are collecting data is to help determine the best strategy for changing negative behavior—not to punish the student.

Step 3

Use the collected data to formulate a summary statement that documents the problem and describes it in some detail. This step will help you integrate the information you have obtained and move toward a solution.

Step 4

Brainstorm some possible solutions to this problem based on the information in your statement. Note anything that sounds good, whether or not you plan to implement it. For each solution you propose, also indicate the outcome you expect.

Return for a moment to the example in Step Two. To deal with the student, Ms. Montoya might consider ignoring him unless he's in his seat (which would probably only make him more persistent), calling on him more often (which might meet his need for attention), allowing him specified conference time (which would probably only work during that specified time), or gluing him to his chair (which would probably get her fired from her job). Noting the probable outcomes will help you decide which solutions to implement.

Step 5

Select one or more proposed solutions to implement. Record the outcomes and, if possible, reassess the situation with the data collection strategies you selected in Step Two.

Ms. Montoya decided to "sell" conference time, and gave the student five paper clips which he placed on his belt. Each paper clip could "buy" her attention when she was working with another student or group. According to the rules, he could interrupt her at any time he needed her, as long as he had one of his paper clips, which he surrendered, one by one, each time he came up to talk to her. She warned him that he would have to decide when it was really important for her to help him, as she would not answer him unless he had a paper clip left. He could ask other class members for help if he wanted. She also made a point of stopping by his desk when he was working independently and reinforcing his positive choices.

Ms. Montoya started giving the student five paper clips for the morning and another five for the afternoon. Within days, he was down to five for the entire day, and then three. Within two weeks, the problem was solved.

Continue testing other possible solutions if your first attempts do not produce satisfactory results. When you test your ideas, you will be making some changes in your behavior, in the environment of the classroom, or in interactive patterns. Keep track of the impact the changes have on the student—good and bad—and evaluate the proposed solution. When necessary, go back to Step Four and think through some more ideas. If you feel stuck, you may want to share the file with your principal, the school counselor, a trusted colleague, or even the student's parents, for additional suggestions.

Step 6

Describe your plans for maintenance and follow-up. You may need to collect more data and implement new solutions from time to time.

CHAPTER NINE

Encouraging Student Responsibility

If asked how they would change their students, most teachers would make them more self-managing and responsible. Few teachers mind filling the cognitive gaps, yet teaching students self-management skills often takes up valuable instructional time.

Some teachers condition their students to act irresponsibly by not recognizing the self-management skills they do have. These teachers assume that students are unable to handle responsibility and that adults must take on much of that responsibility for them. In this way, well-meaning teachers may trap themselves into doing things students could do, or learn to do, thereby preventing the students from experiencing opportunities for growth in these areas.

On the other hand, some teachers are amazed when a lesson fails because the students did not have the self-management skills necessary to complete the task. Student success is often undermined when the activity requires decision making, interactive competence, or other forms of self-management that the students have not yet acquired. Quite naturally, these disasters tend to occur during independent, small-group activities or activities that require students to independently select a task and work alone.

This chapter is based upon the following assumptions:

Students need certain responsible learning (self-management) behaviors to succeed in school.

Students have not necessarily learned these behaviors and may not know how to apply them when they come to your classroom.

Students can be taught responsible learning behaviors. As with any set of behaviors, these are more effectively achieved gradually and with practice.

In an informal survey, several elementary teachers identified a variety of skills and behaviors as necessary for effective learning. The following is the list of behaviors that the teachers in the survey considered important:

INTRAPERSONAL SKILLS AND BEHAVIORS

Pays attention
Exercises self-control
Listens
Uses time constructively
Does work and assignments
Stays with task until complete
Follows directions
Sets personal goals
Reviews work
Takes care of materials
Has command of the language
Works independently
Has pride in progress
Has desire for achievement and success
Meets class standards and teacher expectations
Gives best of self

INTERPERSONAL SKILLS AND BEHAVIORS

Gets along with others
Shares information
Verbalizes with peers and teachers
Asks questions
Helps others
Cooperates; works well in a group
Participates
Respects the rights and property of others

The rest of this chapter will focus on how to help students develop these behaviors and the decision-making skills that are necessary in most learning situations.

Expectations and Abilities

Many proponents of the open classroom concept in the 1960s and 1970s insisted that students had the ability to select meaningful learning experiences. The validity of this viewpoint came under question when teachers experienced the problems that arose from simply turning students loose on a roomful of exciting and stimulating materials. Unfortunately, creativity and curiosity cannot compensate for a lack of self-management skills, and students who were not able to choose activities, care for materials, or work independently were often lost, overwhelmed, and distracted. Most teachers would recognize the futility of assigning algebraic word problems to students who cannot add or subtract, yet how often are teachers tempted to assign complex work contracts to students who fall apart trying to decide which pencil to use?

Sadly, many students come to a classroom from previous experiences—home or school—in which they were offered few opportunities to make decisions that would have any impact on their lives. Conditioned dependency can contribute significantly to failures and frustrations in school, for both the student and the teacher. When adults offer students instruction and opportunities to become responsible, students become more self-reliant.

Encouraging Decision-Making Skills

The ability to make decisions is fundamental to becoming a responsible person. The classroom offers an array of opportunities for students to make decisions and experience the consequences of those decisions.

If your students are exceptionally responsible, and if you are equipped and well organized, then asking the students to select meaningful learning experiences within the parameters of certain rules may be a realistic objective for your particular class. However, if your students have difficulty deciding between two books for independent reading, don't despair. By starting with simple decisions, you can build your students' confidence in their ability to function independently. Eventually, even the most flustered child can learn to become truly self-managing.

Help students who have difficulty in making decisions by offering assistance, setting time limits, or allowing them to change their minds. If their choices will be final for a certain activity or time period, let them know ahead of time. You can build choices into just about any assignment.

The following activities can help you encourage student responsibility. These activities are fairly simple and are designed to give the students confidence in decision making. Some ideas are more appropriate for older children, a few of whom may require practice at even easier decision-making tasks.

Opportunities for Decision Making

You may wish to offer some of these decision-making choices:

- Decide which of two worksheets to do first.
- Decide which two crayons to use in a drawing.
- Decide which two of the three language puzzles to complete.
- Decide which ten math problems to do.
- Decide where to sit for independent reading when given no option to leave once that location has been selected.
- Decide whether to stop talking or to leave the room.
- Decide, in a group, how to share two cookies between three people so that all three people are satisfied with the decision.
- Decide how to arrange certain materials in a display.
- Decide whether to take a one-minute break now or a three-minute break in ten minutes.
- Decide which learning center to visit during self-selection activity time.
- Decide whether to display a drawing or to take it home to share with the family.
- Decide whether or not a skill requires more practice.

CHAPTER TEN

Reinforcing Positive Behavior

When addressing behavior management, teacher training programs tend to emphasize using praise as positive reinforcement and as a means of maintaining discipline. This emphasis discourages negative practices such as yelling, criticizing, or humiliating students. While research has proven the value of positive reinforcement, teachers need to examine how and why they use it.

Several types of positive reinforcement are possible. Activity reinforcement—rewarding a student with a desirable activity—is discussed in detail in the following chapter. Social reinforcement and token reinforcement are presented in this chapter.

Social Reinforcement

Reinforcement is the foundation of operant conditioning, through which individuals gradually develop a particular behavior. The improvement in performing the behavior comes about as a result of reinforcement. A reinforcer can be anything that encourages a behavior to occur again. Social reinforcers include praise, compliments, or attention to a behavior. They may be verbal or nonverbal.

One of the problems with operant conditioning is that the student must give the desired response or action spontaneously before conditioning can begin. Teachers often try to use praise, one type of social reinforcer, in the hope of *eliciting* responses. However, a statement such as, "I like the way Bobby is sitting quietly," is more likely to prolong Bobby's good behavior than get the other students to settle down and imitate Bobby. Positive reinforcement is most effective when used to recognize and reinforce positive behavior. It is not a means of *eliciting* a positive response.

When a teacher uses praise as a way of controlling behavior, students will probably perceive it as dishonest and insincere. Be sure to praise students for their accomplishments.

Using praise can have negative effects on students, particularly in conflict situations. It can block teacher-student communication when it is used to make a student feel better or to deny a problem. When a student does something poorly, a teacher's praise will not improve the behavior. The student will probably feel that the teacher simply does not understand him or her. Praise may also encourage student dependence on the teacher.

Public praise of one student may be interpreted by other students as criticism of them. Students may also become so accustomed to praise that they perceive an absence of praise as criticism. Recognizing a *particular* achievement may be more successful for encouraging self-management than offering general praise.

Reinforcement with Tokens

Another form of positive reinforcement involves the use of tokens. Some tangible reward is offered for the performance of a desired behavior. The reward may be a piece of candy, a sticker, a marble, a poker chip, a gold star, or any item that the student considers valuable. While using tokens can change student behavior quickly, it may not be the most effective long-term strategy. As with incorrect use or overuse of social reinforcers, several dangers exist in using tokens.

One danger is that teachers may be tempted to increase the rewards, causing "token inflation" to occur. Teachers can get caught up in devoting too much time to distributing, recording, and cashing in tokens. Also, students may become dependent on tokens and perceive the absence of a reward as criticism or failure. Dependence on tokens discourages students from working for intrinsic rewards.

Reinforcement with tokens is usually unnecessary under regular classroom conditions. If you use tokens, do so sparingly, decreasing the rewards over time. Tokens can be useful rewards for nighttime reading, returning weekly progress reports, bringing in news clippings, or completing a weekly assignment. They are not recommended for modifying in-class, off-task student behavior, which may be best accomplished through social and activity reinforcement. Candy and gum are not recommended as token reinforcers.

CHAPTER ELEVEN

Contingency Management

In an effort to keep things under control, many teachers, particularly beginning teachers, start the year with a list of rules and a commitment to be firm. The fear of losing control often leads to a belief in the necessity of continual policing. Intervening when students misbehave will occasionally be necessary, but spending the year watching for and responding to negative behaviors won't leave much time for teaching. In addition, such a role will probably leave you feeling that teaching isn't much fun for you or your students.

This chapter examines a positive approach to getting students to do what you want them to do. The strategies rely on the assumption that promising students a positive outcome for completing work, for example, is more effective—and certainly more pleasant—than threatening them with a negative consequence for not doing so. This approach is called *contingency contracting*[1] and is based on the principle that a desired behavior is more likely to occur if it is followed by a reward each time it occurs. The type of reward suggested by contingency management is a form of positive reinforcement called activity reinforcement.

In contingency management, the rewards for a student's positive behavior are activities or events desired by the student. Contingency contracting uses the principles of operant conditioning, which suggest reinforcing "low probability behaviors" (usually what the teacher wants) with "high probability behaviors" (what the student wants).

The critical element in this process is the reinforcer. Since the value of any reinforcer varies from one person to the next, you may want to observe students to discover which activities or materials they select most frequently when given the choice. Interest inventories might also help you select appropriate reinforcers.

Activity Reinforcers

Activity reinforcers might include working in a favorite center, running an errand, reading with a friend, playing with a favorite toy or game, or doing some helping work like filing or grading papers. Regardless of the reinforcer you offer, the student will only be motivated by those that are personally meaningful and worth cooperating for. The object is to make the students' access to the reinforcer contingent upon their completion of a particular task. In this way you are getting the students to do what you require without the use of threats or authority.

[1] L. Homme, *How to Use Contingency Contracting in the Classroom,* 1973.

Management Guidelines

Lloyd Homme suggests the following guidelines regarding the use of reinforcement in contingency management:

The contract payoff (reward) should be immediate.

Initial contracts should call for and reward small approximations (request small, specific, and simple tasks at first). Work toward the ultimately desired performance gradually.

Reward frequently with small reinforcements; they are far more effective than a few large ones.

The contract should call for and reward accomplishments rather than obedience. . . . Reward for accomplishment leads to independence. Reward for obedience leads only to continued dependence on the person to whom the child learns to be obedient.

Reward the performance after it occurs. Present the reinforcer upon the adequate performance of the behavior (pp. 18–19).

The following guidelines describe the characteristics of proper contracting:

The contract must be fair. Try to relate the amount of reward to the amount of performance.

The terms of the contract must be clear. The child must always know *how much* performance is expected of him and *what he can expect as a payoff.*

The contract must be carried out immediately, according to the terms specified in it.

The contract must be positive. The terms of the contract should *contribute* something to the child's experience, rather than take something away from him.

Contracting as a method must be used systematically. The laws of contingency go on working all the time, whether one pays any attention to them or not. Once contracting has been established as a motivation-management procedure, it should be maintained (pp. 19–21).

What about the "morality" of this reward system? Homme explains that although "teachers (and parents) sometimes feel uncomfortable with rewarding students 'for what they should be doing anyhow,' . . . the fact is that children learn better, and more willingly, if reinforcers follow difficult activities" (p. 20).

Motivating with Positive Contingencies

Alex is having a hard time paying attention to his work. He is not disturbing anyone, but he should have been finished a long time ago. What do you do to encourage Alex to do his work? Without considering the possibility of ignoring or accepting Alex's off-task behavior, you have two choices: to offer a reward or a threat. The negative response might be:

"If you're not done in ten minutes, you can't go out for recess."

"If you don't get busy, I'll have to call your mother tonight."

"That does it! You're going to the principal's office right now!"

On the other hand, you might simply turn the first example around and say:

"If you're done in ten minutes, you can go out for recess."

You're saying the same thing, yet in a far more positive way. Now if Alex isn't a big fan of recess, neither statement is likely to work very well. What else do you have to offer?

"Alex, would you run this message to the office as soon as you're done?"

"Why don't you finish up so you can play 'Battleship' with Joshua?"

"If you can finish before the bell, you can use the Teacher's Guide to check your own paper."

The motivation you offer will depend upon the preference of the individual student. Selecting effective reinforcers is easier to do when you have collected data, observed, and interacted with students to learn their preferences.

While the negative response might get Alex back to work, would you rather have him finish his assignment to avoid going to the principal's office or to check his own paper? Clearly, the positive reinforcers are geared more toward developing self-management skills.

CHAPTER TWELVE

Student Behavior and Consequences

The three behavior management techniques presented in this chapter are similar in that they are nonpunitive and nonjudgmental. They are intended to help students see the connection between their behavior and the outcome of their behavior. All three strategies encourage mutual respect between student and teacher and are based on the assumption that students have the right to make independent decisions.

Strategies involving *public criteria, I-messages,* and *logical consequences* are nonauthoritarian and often more effective than "power trips," which can be the cause of much disruption.

Like contingency contracting, these strategies deal with consequences. However, rather than focusing on a student reward which will be given upon the completion of a particular task, these strategies involve helping students see the impact of their behavior on another person, on the class, or on themselves. While useful for eliciting positive behavior, they are also appropriate for intervening in negative student behavior.

Public Criteria

Getting students to cooperate with the dozens of management rules necessary to run a classroom can occupy a large portion of a teacher's time. There are good reasons for the rules and considerations. While it may seem obvious to you why the students need to return reference books in a certain order, put the lids back on the paste jars, put the marbles away when they're done playing, or keep their hands out of the fish tanks, these are often the very behaviors you have to state and explain.

Public criteria are statements made by the teacher that explain why students should behave in a certain way. The reasons for the requested behavior are clearly stated and often explained in terms of consequence on the group, environment, or some object in the environment, rather than being stated as an accusation.

Study the two sets of statements below. Notice how the ones on the left are preferable to those on the right:

"Please put the books back in alphabetical order so they will be easier to find the next time we use them."	*"These books are a mess! Put them back in alphabetical order."*
"Please cover the paste when you are finished so that it will not be dried up when we need to use it again."	*"I told you to put the covers on the paste jars."*
"Please pick up the marbles so that no one slips on them and gets hurt."	*"Please put those marbles away for me."*
"If you take the fish out of the fish tank, they won't be able to breathe."	*"Don't touch the fish tank."*

Note that the examples on the left are not commands. This fact alone may contribute to their effectiveness. In addition, when students cooperate with requests stated as in the examples on the left—those stated in terms of a cause and effect—they are doing so for the benefit of the class, the fish, or themselves. When students cooperate with statements such as those on the right, they are doing so to please the teacher or as a result of the teacher's power.

Public criteria offer a logical reason for doing something, which encourages the development of independence and self-management. Likewise, the likelihood of the student maintaining and repeating the positive behavior without instruction or threats from the teacher is increased.

I-Messages

Public criteria may sometimes be stated in the form of *I-messages.*[1] I-messages tell the student what is happening to the teacher as a result of the student's behavior and are offered as strong alternatives to the accusation of a you-message. Consider the differences in the statements below:

"I can't hear my reading group with all this noise."	*"You are making too much noise."*
"I don't enjoy reading a story when no one seems to be listening."	*"You are being extremely rude."*

Note that the statements on the left do not hold the judgments and negative evaluations that are present in the statements on the right. For this reason, the I-message is less likely to generate a negative response from the student.

Because they focus on the needs of the teacher, I-messages seem to work most effectively when a generally positive relationship already exists between the teacher and student. Stating that something is bothering you won't have much impact unless your students care, at least to a certain degree, about how you feel. This technique provides an excellent alternative to accusing or attacking your students, and is especially effective when stated in terms of the best interest of the group. While I-messages can also foster a positive, open relationship between you and your students, be careful that you are not simply using this technique to manipulate your students.

[1] T. Gordon, *T.E.T., Teacher Effectiveness Training,* 1974.

Logical Consequences

Logical consequences also show the connection between the student's behavior and the outcome of that behavior.[2] As with public criteria, logical consequences are based on rules of order which operate to protect and benefit the group; they are not simply the results of arbitrary, individual decisions.

Stating the logical consequence is helpful particularly when a student is exhibiting some negative behavior.

Because of your devotion to your job, the time you put into planning and preparing, and the fact that you generally care about your students, you may find it difficult not to react emotionally to problems that arise, either out of frustration for having to deal with situations you wish wouldn't occur, or because of a tendency to take conflicts personally (especially when materials you care about are being abused or when you are criticized or verbally attacked). One feature of stating logical consequences is that it allows you to disengage from the emotionalism of a conflict. You can withdraw from the conflict and the child's provocation without withdrawing from the child. Require that the child take responsibility for the consequences of his or her behavior.

Adult disengagement does not mean accepting or ignoring negative behavior. It does, however, preclude fighting with the child, preaching, nagging, threatening, or criticizing, and it also precludes giving in. Disengagement releases you from the role of the punisher, a power role in which you may be angry and judgmental.

[2] R. Dreikurs and L. Grey, *Logical Consequences: A New Approach to Discipline,* 1968.

Your involvement, then, is limited to arranging the consequences by offering choices and helping the student understand the connection between what he or she did and what happened, or will happen, as a result. Imagine that Justin has forgotten his library book. Patrice has been bothering the other students at her table. Maria and Eddie are arguing over a book. Mark just called you "stupid." How do you respond to these situations? You might say:

> *"I'm sorry, Justin. You can take that book out as soon as you return the last one you borrowed."*
>
> *"Patrice, will you please find a place to work alone until lunchtime. You're welcome to work at your table this afternoon if you can do so quietly."*
>
> *"I don't want this book to get damaged. I'll take it until you two resolve the problem of who gets it first."*
>
> *"Mark, we don't call names in this classroom. I'll be happy to talk with you as long as you don't call names."*

In each example, the consequence results from the student's behavior. Explaining the logical consequences puts the responsibility for the problem back on the shoulders of the student who created it. You are able to stand back, without getting angry or involved in the problem, and without solving the problem for the student. You also demonstrate that, while the behavior is unacceptable, the student is still accepted. By doing this, you assume the role of an encourager, one who helps students to grow and realize their potential through successful performance and social integration. You also help your students recognize and select available options, thus fostering their ability to make decisions and predict outcomes.

Whenever possible, let students know ahead of time what the consequences of their actions will be. If you have told Justin that he needs to return his library book by tomorrow in order to sign out another book, then Justin's responsibility for the book is reinforced. Although the students are responsible for their behavior, the logical consequences are arranged by the adult. Your role in arranging the consequences is one of giving choices. Without preaching or moralizing, you are telling the students what they *could* do—not what they should do. With that knowledge, the student becomes responsible for the decision he makes as well as the *immediate* outcome of his choice.

INDEX